insight text guide

Kim Edwards

Romeo and Juliet

William Shakespeare

First published in 2024, reprinted in 2025.

Insight Publications Pty Ltd
3/350 Charman Road
Cheltenham VIC 3192
Australia
Tel: +61 3 8571 4950
Email: books@insightpublications.com.au

www.insightpublications.com.au

William Shakespeare's Romeo and Juliet / Kim Edwards

Kim Edwards asserts the moral right to be identified as the author of this work.

ISBNs:
9781923154728 (print)
9781923154711 (digital)

Cover design by Melisa Paredes
Typesetting by Aptara®, Inc.
Edited by Julia Carlomagno
Proofread by Janice Bird

Printed by Markono Print Media Pte Ltd

Insight Publications acknowledges the Traditional Custodians of the Country on which we meet and work, the Boonwurrung People of the Kulin Nation. We pay our respects to their Elders past and present, and extend that respect to all Aboriginal and Torres Strait Islander peoples.

contents

CHARACTER MAP

OVERVIEW

About the author

Elizabethan writer William Shakespeare is generally regarded as the most famous playwright in the world, and there are hundreds of films and documentaries, thousands of books and scholarly articles, and millions of online words devoted to discussing his life and works – so it is extraordinary how many mysteries there still are about him.

Records from the time of his life are sparse and contradictory, and historians and scholars continue to debate and argue over the possibilities. We think he was born on 23 April 1564, but that is only a guess extrapolated from his baptism certificate. We know he actually died on that same day fifty-two years later, but the cause of death is unknown. He was both born and buried in the English town of Stratford-upon-Avon, but spent much of his life working in London, writing plays that were wildly popular and innovative – although there is no clear information about how he reached that point in his career. Most of his family were probably illiterate; it is likely he only received a basic education (he certainly never went to university); he married at eighteen and had three children – and there is no record of what he then did for a decade, until the success of his plays was suddenly being discussed, critiqued and celebrated by fellow writers in 1592.

His acting company performed frequently for Queen Elizabeth I and her successor, King James I. He was lucky enough to survive the Black Death pandemic, as there were multiple outbreaks of the bubonic plague across Europe during his lifetime. So, when playhouses in London were closed to reduce the spread of disease, he turned his hand to writing poetry, or his theatre company would leave the city to tour the regions.

Although the authorship of some of his writings is under debate, it is generally accepted by scholars that he wrote at least thirty-nine plays, three narrative poems and 154 sonnets. After his death, two of his friends worked together in 1623 to compile drafts, prompt copies (production copies, containing all the technical cues for a performance), actors' transcripts and even pirated versions, to publish a collection of his dramatic works known as the First Folio. They divided the plays into 'comedies', 'histories' and 'tragedies', and their efforts ensured Shakespeare's popularity continued through future generations.

More than 400 years later, scholars and fans still ponder why Shakespeare's characters, stories and language continue to fascinate and resonate with us as modern readers and theatre-goers. There are lots of theories: for example, the universality of Shakespeare's themes, which means his plays can be constantly reinterpreted in new settings, for new cultures and with new diverse casting; or that, despite sounding dense and archaic, his inventive use of language is so evocative it can often sound and feel strangely modern. After all, he did invent hundreds of words for the English language that we still use today. Or perhaps it is because some things never change – we continue to love stories about romance and violence, and action and drama, and twists of fate. In studying *Romeo and Juliet,* we have to prepare ourselves for dangerous street gangs and vicious sword fights, bad jokes and slapstick comedy, passionate love affairs and the revelation of secrets – and shock surprises entwined with impending tragedy.

Synopsis

In the northern Italian city of Verona, the Capulet and Montague families have been feuding for years, so when Juliet, the only child of Lord and Lady Capulet, and Romeo, the sole heir of Lord and Lady Montague, meet accidently at a party and fall in love, the complications are extreme. Unable to confide in friends or family, Romeo goes to Friar Lawrence to ask him to perform a secret marriage, while Juliet enlists the help of the Nurse to enable her to be with Romeo. However, when another street fight breaks out, and Romeo kills Tybalt (a Capulet) in anger at the death of his friend Mercutio, the newlyweds are separated as Romeo is banished from Verona.

During his absence, Juliet is being forced by her parents into an arranged marriage with a young nobleman called Paris, and despairs that she cannot reveal she is already Romeo's wife. She entreats the Friar to help, and he comes up with a complicated plan to fake her death. Romeo hears news of Juliet's 'death' and rushes back to Verona to die beside her – only to be confronted by Paris, whom he also fights and kills.

The Friar arrives in time to see Juliet revive and discover Romeo has already killed himself. Juliet refuses to live without her husband, and when authorities and other family members find both lovers dead, the Friar has to explain what has happened. Lady Montague died of grief when her son was exiled, but Lord Capulet and Lord Montague promise to reconcile finally in united sympathy over their dead children. Prince Escales, the leader of Verona, who failed to stop the family conflict sooner, also grieves his part in this, the loss of his own family members Mercutio and Paris, and the ultimate tragic death of Juliet and Romeo.

Character summaries

Juliet: thirteen years old, the only daughter of Lord and Lady Capulet. Intelligent and resourceful, but falls in love with Romeo, the son of her family's enemy. Marries Romeo in secret with the help of the Nurse and Friar Lawrence, but is being forced to marry Paris by her parents. Kills herself when she finds Romeo poisoned.

Romeo: seventeen years old, the only son of Lord and Lady Montague. Charming, well-reputed, and best friends with Benvolio and Mercutio. Marries Juliet, but ends up killing her cousin Tybalt in revenge for Mercutio's death, and is banished. Returns to Verona upon hearing of Juliet's 'death', kills Paris in self-defence and then poisons himself when he mistakenly believes Juliet is dead.

Benvolio: Romeo's cousin and best friend. Peace-loving and loyal to his family the Montagues, he also tries to help his friends but ends up losing both Romeo and Mercutio during the fight with Tybalt.

Mercutio: best friends with Romeo and Benvolio; related to Prince Escales but supports the Montague family. Witty and reckless; steps in when Romeo refuses to fight Tybalt and is unexpectedly killed.

Tybalt: Juliet's cousin and a proud Capulet. Always seeking conflict with the Montagues despite the counsel of others, which ends with him killing Mercutio and then being killed by Romeo.

Paris: kinsman to Prince Escales, but eager to join the Capulet family by marrying Juliet. After she is discovered 'dead' before their wedding, he challenges Romeo to a fight at her tomb and is killed.

Friar Lawrence: spiritual advisor to both the Capulet and Montague families. Agrees to marry Juliet and Romeo in secret to heal the families' feud, but then must invent a plan to fake Juliet's death to avoid sanctioning bigamy. The only character left at the play's end who knows enough to explain what happened.

The Nurse: Juliet's companion, who has cared for her since she was a baby. Worldly and gregarious – a Capulet employee but treated more like family. Helps facilitate Juliet's secret marriage but then advises giving up Romeo, so loses her role as Juliet's confidante.

Lord Capulet: head of the Capulet household. Domineering but also fickle and easily swayed. Has high aspirations for his daughter Juliet, and becomes abusive when she refuses to marry Paris. Reconciles with his rival, Lord Montague, after the loss of their children.

Lady Capulet: wife of Lord Capulet and mother of Juliet. Skilled at coping with her volatile husband, but does not know her daughter well at all. Is in anguish, at the play's end, when she realises what has happened to her child.

Lord Montague: head of the Montague household. Fond of his wife and only son, but continues to feud with the Capulets, and struggles to understand and relate to Romeo. Ultimately loses his entire family.

Lady Montague: wife of Lord Montague and mother of Romeo. Quiet and protective of her family, dies of grief after Romeo is banished.

Prince Escales: ruler of Verona, with connections to both the Capulet and Montague households. Intelligent and authoritative, but cannot end the ongoing feud. Has the final words in the play.

BACKGROUND & CONTEXT

Elizabethan society

During the reign of Queen Elizabeth I (1558–1603), England enjoyed a renaissance of relative prosperity, power and progress in art and science. Shakespeare's early career success was impacted by the society in which he lived and wrote. Even though his plays are often set in historical times or foreign locations, they present incisive social commentary on contemporary local issues of class, gender, politics and religion.

Social class

Traditional social hierarchy in Elizabethan England was about heritage, wealth and political power. Scholars argue about how to designate the ranks, but in *Romeo and Juliet* five distinct categories are represented.

- Royalty: leaders of society as ordained by God. Prince Escales rules Verona, and his word should be law.
- Nobility: members of the privileged and prestigious upper class, who are born into or granted noble titles such as Count or Lord. The Capulets and Montagues are members of this class.
- Gentry: less powerful members of the upper class, including knights, well-born landowners and merchants, and well-reputed professionals, such as members of the clergy. Friar Lawrence may associate with nobility, but he is not socially of their rank.
- Yeomanry: members of the working middle class; commoners, tradesmen and artisans with independent incomes but no wealth or social lineage. The Apothecary is seen living in poverty, while the Musicians are worried where their next meal will come from.
- Servants and labourers: members of the working lower class; hired help. However, social mobility is available to some, evident in the privilege the Nurse and Balthazar enjoy in working closely with nobility, compared to Lord Capulet's illiterate messenger or the loitering servants in the opening scene.

Patriarchy

Key quote

> 'I know I have the body but of a weak and feeble woman; but I have the heart and stomach of a king ...' (Queen Elizabeth I, quoted in Ridgway 2024)

Elizabethan social power was not only about class and wealth. It was also about gender, as highlighted in Queen Elizabeth I's famous Tilbury speech in 1588. Her assent to the throne posed a contradiction for this patriarchal society, where gender roles were strictly divided. Beyond the monarch herself, women did not have official legal, political or financial rights. They were considered the property of their fathers until they married, whereupon they were subject to the rule of their husbands. Marriage and bearing children were considered a woman's familial, social and religious duty; and laws against women voting, accessing higher education, purchasing property or joining guilds to work, left them little other option.

Women were thus limited to the domestic sphere, their principal roles being wife, mother, nursemaid, housekeeper or – for working-class women – engaging in poorly paid work in jobs such as seamstress, cook or cleaner. There were also social expectations about women's demeanour and behaviour. As they were considered physically and intellectually inferior to men, women were expected to be demure, obedient to male authority and chaste in love. Among the upper social classes, women were confined to their home unless chaperoned.

Queen Elizabeth's rhetoric demeans femininity as inferior to masculinity – at that time, she had to claim male traits in order to assert her right to power. In *Romeo and Juliet*, Shakespeare explores the impact of patriarchy and divisive gender roles on multiple characters and the various ways in which they conform to or rebel against these societal forces. For example:

- Juliet defies her father and desires to choose her own husband
- Romeo is derided as unmanly for his emotions and sensitivities
- the Nurse expresses frank views on sex and female agency
- Lord and Lady Capulet appear to have a fraught relationship.

Religion and astrology

With royalty considered ordained by God, Elizabethan society was fundamentally ruled by the Church. Religious leaders could wield great political power and attain high social status. It was necessary to appear pious to be well-respected, so forming associations with your spiritual advisor was good for both your soul and your social aspirations.

However, the Elizabethans were also strongly superstitious, and pagan beliefs in fortune-telling, divination and omens were still influential. In fact, astrology (interpretating how celestial bodies influence human fate) was highly respected as a scholarly discipline, uniting the science of astronomy with the divine and mystical. Queen Elizabeth even employed a famous astrologer as her advisor. Studying the heavens to understand destiny and predict the future was thus not considered to be at odds with religious beliefs. However, in *Romeo and Juliet*, key characters wrestle with the dilemma of whether:

- their path is destined by the stars and/or God's will
- exerting their own free will is a righteous or irreligious act
- the choices they make are destiny or their own responsibility.

Elizabethan theatre

Romeo and Juliet was probably first performed in London in 1597, and – as with all his plays – Shakespeare had to craft his work to fit the space and suit his audience.

Traditional Elizabethan theatres had several tiers of seating, surrounding a platform stage that extended out from a roofed building into the central 'yard', which was open to the weather. 'Groundlings' would pay a pittance to stand in the yard and watch up close, while wealthy theatre patrons would pay for seats at a dignified distance in the upper levels. Shakespeare was therefore catering for an audience literally ranging from the 'lowest' members of his society to the 'highest', and his plays always feature both working-class characters and nobility, portraying experiences from all walks of life.

Even so, with performances four or five hours long, theatre patrons could become loud and disruptive. Although modern theatre productions tend to encourage respectful viewers, Shakespeare's audiences were drinking, buying snacks from vendors, heckling actors or even hooking up during performances. Keeping a rowdy crowd's attention meant including plenty of drama, comedy and action, and with no amplification, dialogue was presented in a loud declamatory style and often repeated key information to ensure everyone heard important plot, character and setting details.

Describing locations was especially important, as Elizabethan theatre traditionally included little or no stage scenery and no artificial lighting, and performances were held in the daytime. Therefore, setting the scene with atmospheric dialogue was essential to help the audience visualise dark nights, violent storms or delicate sunrises.

Although Shakespeare often set his plays in exotic places and historical eras, his actors wore contemporary clothes regardless. Modern productions often follow this trend to indicate how such stories continue to relate to a modern world. Shakespearean costuming was still lavish and colourful, especially for noble characters – although this was technically breaking Elizabethan law, as you were not meant to wear clothes outside your social class, and actors were not affluent or even highly respected in society.

It was also illegal for women to perform on stage, so all Elizabethan actors were male. Young boys whose voices had not yet broken played the serious female characters, while men in drag performed the comical roles of older women. Acting troupes thus included a variety of male performers playing the same sorts of roles in each new production.

Small casts with fewer actors meant better wages for each performer and greater efficiency in taking a production on the road. As a result, Shakespeare's plays often have roles that can be doubled – an actor plays one role for several acts, then turns up as a different character later. Some performers played multiple roles, and Shakespeare sometimes had crowd scenes, battles or even major deaths take place offstage because there were not enough cast members to depict all the characters.

This does not mean Shakespeare's plays were not theatrical spectacles, though – his audience needed to be kept entertained! Musicians played character songs, dance numbers or sound effects from above, below or alongside the stage. The main platform included trapdoors through which performers could appear or disappear, while doorways and balconies at the back of the stage afforded spaces for supernatural or spying characters to listen and lurk.

Then there were the special effects. Shakespearean plays utilised stage props in abundance – weapons, live animals, plants, furniture, and lanterns, candles or flaming torches were often used. Smoke was wafted onstage to portray cannon fire or eerie fog. Cannon balls were rolled backstage to emulate the sound of thunder, fireworks lit for battle effects, ropes and pulleys used to fly in magical beings. The elegant and stylised use of red silk for blood was an option, but fake limbs, blood packs and animal parts were also available for more gruesome stage violence.

The impact of Elizabethan theatre can be seen in the key themes of Shakespeare's plays:

- social commentary and contrasting social classes
- misunderstood or misinterpreted speeches or messages
- doubling, disguise and mistaken identity
- conflicts between old historical traditions and new, modern ideas.

Romeo and Juliet: performance and publication

The text of *Romeo and Juliet* has a complicated past. There is no definitive version of Shakespeare's works because he wrote scripts to be performed, not preserved. His handwritten originals, or 'holographs', likely became stage managers' working scripts, worn and dog-eared, full of notes and amendments. His actors would have copied out the sections they were in, and these individual scripts would also have been edited and altered as plays were rehearsed, revised, performed and toured.

Such was the popularity of Shakespeare, though, that his works were constantly pirated. Without copyright protection laws in that era, unauthorised versions of his plays would be cobbled together from actors' sections or memory and printed for sale. The First Quarto ('quarto': a small, cheap, flimsy book) of *Romeo and Juliet* was published in 1597, and the Second Quarto (Q2) in 1599. Q1 is far shorter and missing famous speeches that appear in later versions. Q2 is considered by many scholars as most likely based on Shakespeare's holograph, so modern editions often use this version. A Third and Fourth Quarto were edited reprints of Q2, until Shakespeare's colleagues collaborated after his death to publish a version of the play in the collected works of the First Folio in 1623. It proclaimed to be 'Published according to the True Original Copies' and is also a regular choice for modern play editions.

What this means for recent scholars, performers and students is that different versions of the play can have different line numbers, language and punctuation, which can lead to different interpretations when reading the text. Moreover, although his works were written in 'modern' English, after 400 years some words and allusions Shakespeare uses have lost meaning or changed connotation, which makes his works even more challenging to read and understand. Finally, Shakespeare's plays were not actually written to be published – they were only written to be performed, and thus seen and heard.

Reading and studying *Romeo and Juliet* is therefore best supported by:

- choosing a well-reputed, annotated edition
- exploring context
- considering a variety of interpretations
- reading aloud or listening to audio versions
- seeing film adaptations or live performances.

GENRE, STRUCTURE & LANGUAGE

The genre of tragedy

In his *Poetics*, ancient Greek philosopher Aristotle argued for tragedy as the epitome of art. He claimed a work of tragedy must be about issues of import, told in elevated and expressive language, evoking profound emotions and creating tragic pleasure ('catharsis') for an audience:

> Tragedy is an imitation of an action that is admirable, complete and processes magnitude; in language made pleasurable ... effecting through pity and fear the purification of such emotions. (Aristotle cited in 1996, p.10)

Although tragedy as a genre continued to evolve, the expectation of profundity, intellect, sophisticated language and strong emotion continued, as did expectations about character and plot. Characters must be noble and virtuous but flawed in their humanity. Moreover, to evoke pity and fear, such characters must experience a terrible misfortune – often by making a relatable mistake – and thus come to represent human suffering. It is an edifying genre that offers views on morality: by the end of a tragedy, something new should be understood about the human condition, and a new order – personal, familial, social or political – should be established.

Although Shakespeare's plays are traditionally categorised into 'tragedies', 'comedies' and 'histories', his works are always reconsidering and reimagining genre tropes and expectations. The plot events of *Romeo and Juliet* adhere to the general expectation of a tragedy in the needless loss of young lives. However, the play tempers elegant, sophisticated language with vulgarity, and emotional scenes that encourage pity and fear with raucous comic moments. Some noble characters are revealed to be far from admirable, and some ignoble characters prove to have nuanced and delicate sensibilities. Yet, recognising flawed but lovable characters experiencing suffering they do not deserve, and considering what this reveals about the human experience and what lessons may be learnt, remains central to an appreciation of *Romeo and Juliet*.

Structure

The tradition of dividing a play into five sections called 'acts' also came from ancient Greek theatre. An 'act' in theatre designates a key sequence of plot events, but in *Romeo and Juliet* the divisions are conventional rather than functional, as the action often flows across from one section to the next, and modern productions make different choices about where to place intervals during the play. Each of the five acts is divided up into scenes – a change of scene indicates a significant change of place.

For the purpose of performance and study, Shakespeare's plays are numbered by line. As his dialogue is often in blank verse (poetry with metre but not rhyme), his works are measured in lines like poetry rather than in sentences or paragraphs. The shorthand for quotations indicates act, scene and line(s), e.g. '2.2.33–6' refers to Act 2, Scene 2, lines 33 to 36.

Within these structural divisions Shakespeare uses other playwriting conventions and literary techniques. *Romeo and Juliet* opens with a famous Prologue, an introductory speech functioning as backstory or a preview of the action. It is spoken by the Chorus – an individual or group narrating from outside the action of the play. It also ends with a speech by the Prince that functions as an epilogue, reflecting on what has occurred and what may happen next. The Prince, a figure of public authority, addresses both the characters and the audience.

Shakespeare often experiments with these conventional script elements in innovative and dynamic ways. In *Romeo and Juliet*, structural components of the play work to foreshadow and build tension towards the tragic ending, but this is strategically balanced with delay and surprise: key events occur at unexpected moments, and important action or information is deferred by the intrusion of comical or apparently less significant scenes.

Moreover, Shakespearean plays often explore the conceit of performance itself. The audience sees and hears 'private' interactions that are not meant to be witnessed by other characters. In Elizabethan theatres, boundaries between public and private space were ambiguous, with numerous points of access between performers' and audience areas, and the groundlings within reach of the stage. This inspires questions about who is performing and declaiming within the world of the play, and who is eavesdropping on whom. Thus *Romeo and Juliet* also has delicate interplay with the parts of dramatic speech, including:

- **dialogue** – conversations between characters
- **monologue** – a speech said aloud by one character
- **soliloquy** – an inner monologue in which one character shares their thoughts and feelings with the audience
- **aside** – a secret remark from one character, only heard by the audience.

Shakespearean language

Given the complications of staging in Elizabethan theatre, plays needed to give vivid descriptions, reiterate ideas and key information in memorable ways, and establish characters through style and vocabulary. Thus, Shakespeare's works are characterised by dynamic and creative uses of figurative language, including symbolism and motifs, and varied language styles, indicating class, status or personality.

A well-known characteristic of Shakespearean language is the use of the personal pronouns 'thee', 'thou', 'thine', 'thy' and 'thyself' (following the pattern of 'me', 'I', 'mine', 'my' and 'myself'). 'You' was once reserved for formal address, whereas 'thou' (*th+ow*) was for more informal and casual conversations. But by the Elizabethan era, this distinction was falling out of fashion: 'you' became the default. The archaic informal pronouns 'thee' and 'thou' became assigned to the language of the theatre as another way to designate class, character or tone.

In Shakespeare's plays, 'you' usually indicates formality and equality of status in conversations between upper- or middle-class characters. Meanwhile, 'thee/thou' can represent:

- informality and equality of status between lower-class characters
- class difference when social superiors are speaking to someone of lower rank
- disdain or disrespect if someone is wrongly addressed informally
- affection if high-ranked characters are intimate enough to privately call one another by casual pronouns.

Poetic conventions also aid characterisation in Shakespeare's plays. In *Romeo and Juliet*, **rhyming verse** is employed for the Prince's speeches, giving a sense of gravity and formality, and also for the moments when Romeo and Juliet speak in sonnets together, indicating their harmony. Meanwhile, upper-class characters such as Lord and Lady Capulet and Lord Montague speak in elegant **blank verse** (where the lines have poetic metre and thus sound measured, musical and flowing), whereas working-class figures such as the servants in Act 1, Scene 1 speak in more casual, natural-sounding **prose**.

Many admire Shakespeare's use of figurative language and symbolism – particularly his skill in creating vivid imagery from evocative words loaded with multiple meanings, then repurposing those images and words throughout the play. One example is the lament 'Where civil blood makes civil hands unclean' (Prologue, line 4). 'Civil' here means both polite and courteous, and related to local citizens/civilians. Conflict between the Montague and Capulet households is represented by blood and hands – the multiple connotations of 'civil' suggest the juxtaposition of aristocratic bloodlines and handshakes, with violent, bloodied fists. This exposes the irony of 'noble' families, meant to be dignified and civilised, debasing themselves by 'getting their hands dirty'. The symbolism of hands and blood representing a clash between noble intentions and succumbing to ignoble violence then recurs throughout the play.

SCENE-BY-SCENE ANALYSIS

Prologue

Summary: *The play opens with a poem outlining key plot events. Two families have been feuding for years, but two young people from these opposing households will fall in love. This relationship will end with their deaths, but also finally end the conflict.*

The Prologue is designed to calm an unruly audience and build anticipation but also to set the mood for the performance to come. The opening speech is a perfect sonnet: an elegant and sophisticated poetic form. The musicality of rhythm and rhyme and nuanced use of language establishes a respect for poetic and tragic conventions, and an expectation of a dramatic and serious work to follow.

This speech also introduces the core tensions and conflicts we are about to encounter. These households are meant to be dignified, but resort to violence. Their children should be enemies, but become lovers. The resulting deaths are tragic, but they end the civil unrest.

Act 1

1.1 Summary: *A violent street brawl breaks out between Capulets and Montagues, only ceasing when Prince Escales arrives to outlaw such disturbances. Concerned about his son, Romeo, Lord Montague asks his nephew Benvolio to find out what is troubling him; Benvolio discovers his friend has been rejected in love.*

After the Prologue promised noble families and tragic romance, this first scene offers a jarring contrast. Bad puns about sex and violence between Capulet servants heralds a foolish encounter with Montague servants. The resultant sparring is broken up by Benvolio but escalates into a dangerous fight with the arrival of Tybalt. The servants may be from enemy households but seem alike in their taunts and bravado, while their upper-class counterparts have contrasting attitudes to conflict:

Benvolio desires peace and Tybalt is set on violence. The two lords share a mutual animosity and want to attack each other on sight, while their wives attempt to prevent them. The Prince appears powerful and authoritative but, given the duration of this 'ancient' feud, the success of his new pronouncement seems dubious.

Later, Lord Montague and Benvolio are mutually concerned about Romeo, but while his father does not 'know ... nor can learn of' (1.1.135) what is causing Romeo angst, his cousin is more confident he can find out: 'I'll know his grievance or be much denied' (1.1.148). Benvolio and Romeo are both Montagues, peers in age and class, and best friends – but hold contrary views about love and women. Benvolio sympathises with his friend's unrequited crush on Rosaline but suggests he simply 'Examine other beauties' (1.1.219), while Romeo insists with unconscious irony, 'thou canst not teach me to forget' (1.1.228) Rosaline on the eve before he is to meet Juliet.

Key point

The first scene establishes this will not simply be a love story, and the oppositions at work in this play are not going to be straightforward binaries. Complex comparisons and contrasts are already being drawn between social roles, social classes, gender, generations and individuals.

Key vocabulary

'bite my thumb': place a thumb behind the top teeth and flick it out; an insulting and provocative gesture to an enemy.

importuned: asked persistently.

profaners: those who treat something reverent with contempt; the Prince implies that the Capulets and Montagues have violated their swords by staining them with the blood of their neighbours.

Q Why might Shakespeare have chosen to open the play with an interaction between minor characters?

1.2 Summary: *Young, ambitious Paris is eager to marry Juliet, but Lord Capulet reiterates that she is too young and instead invites him to a party with her that evening. The servant delivering the invitations cannot read the guest list, and asks for help from Romeo as the young noble is passing by, giving Benvolio a daring idea.*

Lord Capulet and Paris are discussing male pursuits of their era and class – sociopolitical affairs and acquiring wives. Like Paris, the audience is yet to meet Juliet, but here we first learn about her 'value' as a commodity in this patriarchal society – a count related to the Prince desires her, and Lord Capulet rests all hopes for allegiance and lineage on his only surviving child. Capulet also intimates he is committed to keeping the peace after that royal decree, despite his earlier bravado, and implies he is a caring father protective of his daughter's youth and innocence – however, his would-be son-in-law is the Prince's kinsman, and thus a man worth impressing.

Capulet's illiterate messenger further reinforces class differences in Verona, but also represents a first crucial moment that hangs upon improbable chance or the machinations of 'fate'. That it should be Romeo from whom he seeks help, and that this inspires Benvolio's plan to 'cure' Romeo by viewing other women (paralleling Capulet's suggestion to Paris), sets in motion the plot events foretold in the Prologue. Benvolio's scheme is going to work – but ironically, only in giving his friend a new love interest.

Q What does this scene show us about class and gender roles in the world of the play?

1.3 Summary: *The Nurse reminisces about Juliet's childhood, but Lady Capulet wants to talk about the future. She tells her daughter to think about marrying soon and praises Paris – but Juliet only agrees to meet and consider him as a suitor.*

This scene forms a counterpoint to the previous one by giving an exclusively female perspective on marriage, children and who is in a position to dictate Juliet's future. The setting has changed from outside, the public world, to inside, a private domestic space: a shift from male to female spheres, and from social and political concerns to personal and emotional interactions.

However, even here Juliet has no agency in the decisions being made about her life. She is mostly silent and then ignored or overlooked when finally able to reply; the scene becomes a commentary on her age as well as her gender. An arranged marriage affords an alliance of significant benefit for the Capulet family as a whole so is not deemed a personal decision to be entrusted to a thirteen-year-old girl.

Key vocabulary

Lammas-tide: a Christian celebration of the wheat harvest that occurs on 1 August; Juliet's birthday is on Lammas-eve, 31 July.

Q Compare the respective introductions to the play's title characters in this scene and Scene 2. What do we learn about Romeo and Juliet?

1.4 Summary: *Mercutio and Benvolio are making merry plans to gatecrash the Capulet party, but Romeo is reluctant. Mercutio dismisses his forebodings with a tale about a fairy queen delivering fanciful dreams, until Romeo gives in and enters the party with his friends.*

In introducing the final member of this young male trio, new friendship dynamics are revealed: Benvolio makes careful plans while Mercutio is witty and irreverent, but Romeo, at odds with his friends, is anxious. Romeo is eager to analyse his bad dream, yet Mercutio insists his fairy story demonstrates dreams are 'but vain fantasy' (1.4.98). Although Romeo complains he 'talk'st of nothing' (1.4.96), the audience understands that Mercutio's fantastical tale functions on multiple levels. It introduces Mercutio as comedic but also intelligent and creative, and offers a perspective on the play's motif of dreaming and key themes of love and fate. It also speculates on the importance of language and storytelling – does Mercutio indeed speak of 'nothing', or does his narrative have significance beyond a lighthearted fairytale? The notion of stories or warnings being misinterpreted or misrepresented is foreshadowed here.

Q What motivates Mercutio to deliver his monologue?

1.5 Summary: *Servants finish party preparations as Lord Capulet welcomes his guests. Romeo sees Juliet and is besotted, while Tybalt recognises him but is prevented from intervening by the host. Juliet and Romeo have only a few moments together before Juliet is called away, whereupon they discover each other's identity.*

'Love at first sight' is a romantic notion, but it is fundamentally problematic as it relies upon superficial physical attraction. Romeo is at the party to see Rosaline, but he approaches Juliet because he 'ne'er saw true beauty till this night' (1.5.52). This exposes his capriciousness in love, suggesting that his earlier angst over Rosaline was melodramatic. Yet their interaction has greater importance. Juliet and Romeo's first conversation forms a perfect sonnet. They literally make poetry together when they talk: their words combine in rhyme and synchronise in rhythm. Moreover, their lines balance – they listen carefully to each other's words and respond specifically and in equal amounts, in contrast to Romeo's earlier self-absorbed verbosity and Juliet's experience with censorship. Their flirty discussion is witty and erudite: Romeo asks to kiss Juliet's divine hand; Juliet jokes that hands aren't that holy. Romeo asks about lips, which Juliet quips are for praying, so Romeo prays to kiss her lips instead, and Juliet agrees to share in that 'sin' (1.5.107). Their verbal interaction demonstrates synergy and mutual respect – Romeo is still entranced by her beauty but is discovering more reasons to love her, while Juliet is charmed by his eloquence but also sees through his charm to something more substantial.

They are interrupted (perhaps deliberately) by the Nurse and then Benvolio – the broken prose conversations, where Juliet and Romeo each learn the identity of the stranger they kissed, serve to represent the disruptions their new love will cause in this society.

Key point

'You kiss by th' book' (1.5.109) might mean any of the following.

- Romeo is an experienced, satisfying kisser who has studied this skill!
- He kisses chastely and respectfully as a good Bible-reading boy.
- His kisses are boring and conventional because he sticks to the 'rule book'.

All interpretations open up new possibilities for understanding Juliet as intelligent, discerning and willing to speak her mind, and for considering what sort of character growth Romeo might experience during the course of the play.

Q What do the conversations in this scene reveal about class and intergenerational difference, and contrasts between public, performative speeches and private, intimate dialogue?

Act 2

2.1 Summary: *Romeo avoids his friends and climbs back over the Capulet wall to look for Juliet. Thinking their friend is still pining for Rosaline, Benvolio is sympathetic, while Mercutio is tired and impatient to go home.*

The band of three is down to two: Romeo absents himself from his friends and their discussions about love, sex and women, in pursuit of something he considers more meaningful – to 'find [his] centre out' (2.1.2). Mercutio continues his rant about romance versus sex, but his scepticism and 'tough-love' solutions to what he considers Romeo's problems are countered by Benvolio's concern and sympathy for his friend. Moreover, Benvolio is perceptive enough to realise that Romeo is actually avoiding them rather than sulking, and therefore respectful enough to leave him to it.

Q How are depictions of masculinity and views on love contrasted and compared in this scene?

2.2 Summary: *Seeing Juliet, Romeo admires her beauty and overhears her concerns about loving a Montague. He interrupts her musing, and they talk seriously about their dangerous situation, passionately about their new-found love and playfully when making plans to confirm their wedding the next day.*

Romeo sees Juliet above him at her window, so staging the lovers' interaction is about navigating the literal distance between them. We can contemplate what that space represents – Juliet, spied upon, vulnerable and isolated, like a princess in a tower; Romeo gazing up at a sun goddess, worshipping in submission. However, Juliet also has the strategic high ground in this ambush, and Romeo is legitimately putting his life at risk in trespassing. The distribution of power in this relationship is already unusual: in this patriarchal world Romeo should be in control, but Juliet is shown to have the upper hand, rejecting Romeo's grandiose proclamations of love in favour of a more profound and practical discussion of how their relationship could work. This scene, although often performed emphasising its romantic and poetic language, also has the capacity to be comedic and endearing: the Nurse's constant interruptions create something like an amusing phone conversation when neither party wants to hang up on the other.

Key vocabulary

afeard: afraid.

'O Romeo, Romeo, wherefore art thou Romeo?': famously one of the play's most misunderstood quotes; parodies often show Juliet looking out longingly for her new love because they presume that 'wherefore' means 'where', but it actually means 'why'. She is not asking where Romeo is, she is contemplating *why* she had to fall in love with *him,* of all people.

Q What does the audience learn about the different personalities of Romeo and Juliet as they get to know each other?

2.3 Summary: *Friar Lawrence is working in his herb garden as day dawns. He is unimpressed to hear Romeo has a new love interest in Juliet, but rather unexpectedly agrees to conduct their wedding ceremony that very day anyway.*

Friar Lawrence is initially presented as a wise, trustworthy figure in this society: showing concern for the moral wellbeing of young people under his spiritual care, but also having a religious and political interest in resolving Verona's conflict by reconciling the feuding families. His monologue introduces this theme of individual versus social problems by considering humanity's dependence upon the Earth for life or death, then expanding on the idea using a flower he picks. The plant can both poison and heal, and the Friar muses this is like the two 'opposèd kings' (2.3.27) of good and evil, vying for power within each individual.

This notion of moral complexity develops in the Friar's conversation with Romeo. His good-natured worry that the young man is sleeping around is replaced by concern at Romeo's romantic fickleness. He counsels 'they stumble that run fast' (2.3.94) but immediately agrees to perform the marriage ceremony – the Friar does not practise everything he preaches. With the complex interplay of individual and social concerns, his motivations may prove more complicated than the well-intentioned acts of a simple, godly man.

Q Why does Friar Lawrence agree to marry Romeo and Juliet, despite believing Romeo to have fallen in love again too quickly?

2.4 Summary: *Mercutio and Benvolio look for Romeo again, hoping to find him before Tybalt can. The friends reunite and Mercutio makes crass jokes about love, until the Nurse arrives to question Romeo privately before she informs Juliet of his marriage plans.*

Mercutio's witty but vulgar insults about Tybalt's fighting skills, Romeo's romancing, and the Nurse undermine the serious problems of a secret marriage and threatened duel. Young male culture in Verona is prone to flippant talk of sex and violence: Mercutio and Benvolio's sexist, ageist and fat-shaming treatment of the Nurse (which Romeo is eager to excuse) is particularly unpalatable for modern audiences. Romeo's comparative politeness and respect to the stranger does imply we are not meant to admire his friends' behaviour, however – Romeo unexpectedly exhibits a maturity and civility seemingly uncommon among men his age.

Key vocabulary

anon: soon.

scurvy knave: a mean or despicable young man.

shrived: absolved for one's sins after confession; a rite often undertaken before marriage.

Q Why doesn't Romeo tell his best friends about his new love and plans to marry?

2.5 Summary: *Juliet frets that the Nurse is taking a long time to return with news, then struggles to subdue her frustration when her companion delays delivering the message. She finally hears that Romeo is waiting at Friar Lawrence's place, ready to marry her, and she hurries away.*

Juliet's opening monologue shows her waiting alone, impatient to confirm Romeo's commitment, for 'three long hours' (2.5.11). She compares the speed of thoughts to the slow pace of the Nurse, and is eager to be reunited with her 'sweet love' (2.5.14) despite her previous concerns about this relationship being too hasty. The Friar cautioned Romeo about falling in love too quickly, but here Juliet acknowledges this as characteristic of youth: hot-blooded young love must be fast, in contrast with 'old folks', who are 'Unwieldy, slow, heavy, and pale as lead' (2.5.16–17).

Youth versus age, action versus inaction, recklessness versus thinking, and love versus rationality: the ideas Juliet ponders are key themes also affecting the plot and the significance of this scene. When the Nurse arrives, she seems reluctant to share her news. Juliet tells her that her excuse 'Is longer than the tale thou dost excuse' (2.5.34), and the Nurse's delays not only keep Juliet from her desire, but keep the audience in suspense as well.

Q Why do you think the Nurse takes so long to tell Juliet what she wants to know?

2.6 Summary: *Friar Lawrence hopes this risky marriage will end well, but Romeo is concerned with the present and does not care what dangers the future may bring. Juliet arrives: the lovers kiss, speak of love and exit with the Friar to be wed.*

The Friar worries 'violent delights have violent ends' (2.6.9) and cautions Romeo to 'love moderately' (2.6.14) – but then hurries the young couple away to 'make short work' (2.6.35) of their marriage ceremony. The relationship between violence and love, and the tension between circumspection and recklessness, are key interests in this scene, in which Romeo challenges 'love-devouring Death' to 'do what he dare' (2.6.7) and Juliet explains her 'true love is grown to such excess' (2.6.33) she cannot describe it.

The idea of this relationship spiralling out of control, beyond anyone's ability to pause or rationalise, is at odds with our knowledge of the characters here. The Friar wishes to stop the conflict in Verona – but also to prevent his charges from having premarital sex. Romeo will happily risk death for 'one short minute' (2.6.5) with Juliet, despite knowing their union may endanger them and exacerbate the feud. Juliet insisted only the previous night that their union was 'too rash, too unadvised, too sudden' (2.2.118), but she is now ready to wed the very next day.

Key point

Tragedy as a genre includes good characters making poor choices with terrible results, but there is also tragedy in inevitable events where there was no avoiding a disastrous outcome. The end of Act 2 skips over staging the happy wedding to leave us wondering whether this union is the product of destiny or bad decisions, and worrying about the personal and social impact to come.

Q The Friar describes rash love as explosive: two opposing elements, such as fire and gunpowder, touching only to destroy themselves and their surroundings. How does this imagery relate to other events, characters and themes?

Act 3

3.1 Summary: *Benvolio and Mercutio encounter Tybalt, still seeking Romeo after the party. Romeo tries to avoid a fight, but Mercutio is stabbed and dies. In fury, Romeo kills Tybalt to avenge his friend and must flee, leaving Benvolio to explain. The Prince banishes Romeo.*

Benvolio notes, 'now, these hot days, is the mad blood stirring' (3.1.4): the action is heating up, emotions are heightened and the stakes are higher. Unlike the opening fight, it is now main characters who threaten one another, motivated by fresh complications. Tybalt was told by Lord Capulet to overlook Romeo's intrusion and heard the Prince's decree that street violence is now punishable by death – yet asserts 'injuries / That thou hast done me' (3.1.59–60) warrant a public duel with Romeo now. He is driven beyond reason to uphold honour and exact revenge, but his actions are morally dubious when Romeo insists 'I never injuried thee' (3.1.61). Only the audience knows he loves Tybalt 'better than thou canst devise' (3.1.62) because they are now in-laws.

Key point

The murder of Mercutio, a dynamic, popular character, is unexpected: he dies before the play is even half over. The shock of this death helps the audience to understand Romeo's distress and his irrational decision to take vengeance. Only after Benvolio's cautious monologue, interpreting the situation, do the audience and the play's other characters have the chance to consider the ramifications of the decisions and actions taken in this scene.

Q Who or what should be blamed for Mercutio's death, and why?

3.2 Summary: *Juliet, yearning for her wedding night, is horrified when the Nurse brings news of Tybalt's murder and Romeo's exile. She struggles with conflicting emotions, but agrees when the Nurse promises to smuggle Romeo into her room for a first and final night together.*

Juliet's soliloquy invites parallels to Romeo's earlier imagery – she also considers him a light in the darkness, and imagines his face illuminating the heavens. However, he compared her to dawning sun outshining the moon, and she envisions him as night stars more beautiful than the sun. Once more their words and mutual understanding balance and complement each other: they value and love the other more than themselves.

In contrast with Romeo's romanticising, however, Juliet is thinking practically and physically – she longs not just for nightfall and Romeo, but for her wedding night. Unlike Romeo's mythologising of her as a divine object, or Mercutio and the Nurse's vulgar claims about what 'love' reduces to, Juliet's yearning here unites sex and love: where 'strange love [can] grow bold', in privacy and intimacy it becomes 'true love acted [in] simple modesty' (3.2.15–16). She offers a more emotionally mature consideration of love in marriage, but her musing on heavenly and earthly pleasures is interrupted by traumatic news, provoking her unanticipated reactions.

Q How does Juliet describe Romeo, and why?

3.3 Summary: *Friar Lawrence informs Romeo that the Prince has banished him, and Romeo despairs as the Friar tries to reason with him. The Nurse arrives and tells of Juliet's grief, which increases Romeo's distress, until the Friar lectures him fiercely and advises him to go to Juliet at once.*

The Friar dubs Romeo ungrateful, unreasonable and unmanly, but everything he has loved is now in jeopardy: Mercutio died blaming him; he has killed Tybalt and is now exiled from all he has ever known; he may never see his new wife again. Death seems more merciful to him than living in banishment, which we fear has arrived when there is an unknown knock and Romeo refuses to hide. The Nurse's description of Juliet's constant weeping gives the audience the impression of an overwrought, distraught young bride, while the Friar insults, reasons with and orders Romeo to 'get thee to thy love' (3.3.146), before Romeo will take comfort. The Friar suggests that the best solution to the situation is for Romeo to flee to Mantua and wait there, promising implausibly to 'find a time' to fix everything: 'blaze your marriage, reconcile your friends, / Beg pardon of the Prince' (3.3.150–2).

Key vocabulary

blaze: announce.

Q What are the motivations of the Friar and the Nurse in this scene?

3.4 Summary: *Tybalt's death has delayed discussion of Paris' marriage with Juliet, but Lord Capulet decides to organise their wedding for next Thursday anyway. He tells his wife to let their daughter know.*

Lord Capulet's unexpected change of heart about Juliet's wedding to Paris marks a shift in attitude: Juliet's age and consent are no longer important, as he now insists 'she will be ruled' (3.4.13) by him. His new eagerness to solidify an alliance with Paris suggests the extent to which his convictions have been threatened by recent events. Despite his resolve not to 'revel much' (3.4.26) after Tybalt's murder, he is intent on organising a wedding within days of his nephew's death. At his party Capulet was concerned about social niceties, so this change in his approach is significant.

Q What personal, political or social motivations are influencing Capulet's sudden decision?

3.5 Summary: *After their wedding night together, dawn breaks far too quickly for the lovers. Romeo must leave, just as Lady Capulet arrives to inform her daughter she is to marry Paris. Juliet refuses, and Lord Capulet threatens to disown her if she does not obey.*

The lovers' dialogue continues to show the equality of their relationship as they make concessions, compromise and show respect for each other's needs and opinions. This time, however, Juliet demonstrates more impulsivity, encouraging Romeo by saying, 'stay yet, thou need'st not to be gone' (3.5.16), while Romeo is more circumspect, knowing that he 'must be gone' (3.5.11) as his life depends on it. There is a new maturity to their relationship, an understanding of the complexities of their situation, in contrast to the idealism that permeated their earlier conversations. This adds further poignancy to their parting.

The ensuing interactions reinforce Juliet's struggle for agency over her life. A married woman now, she deceives her mother by agreeing Romeo is a villain and claiming her tears are for Tybalt, then emphatically refuses to marry Paris. The reactions of those around her are disappointing: the Nurse and her mother both try to subdue Lord Capulet in his furious threats of violence and exile at her disobedience, but ultimately Lady Capulet capitulates – 'Do as thou wilt, for I have done with thee' (3.5.203) – and the Nurse praises Paris over Romeo and advises bigamy. Juliet, desolate, recognises she has lost all family and friends in staying true to her chosen love, but reasons that, if the Friar will not help her, she will 'have power to die' (3.5.242).

Key vocabulary

nightingale: a bird that sings at night; Juliet hopes she hears 'the nightingale' (3.5.2) as this means that Romeo can stay longer.

tidings: news.

Q What plot points and key issues are deliberately left unresolved at the end of Act 3?

Act 4

4.1 Summary: *Paris tries to speak with Juliet of love and marriage, but her responses are ambiguous. When he leaves, Juliet threatens to kill herself if Friar Lawrence does not help her escape marrying Paris. The Friar hurriedly invents a complicated plan for Juliet to fake her own death.*

Juliet continues to exhibit unexpected skill at subterfuge and manipulation. She does not lie to Paris, but allows him to think she will abide by his wedding plans. Accordingly, her distraught outburst and threats of suicide to Friar Lawrence may be genuine, but it is also possible she is using guilt to manipulate him into doing what she wants. There is more at stake for her than a life with Romeo – we know what would happen if her father discovers her deception, so she is risking her family, reputation and very life.

The Friar's plan unfolds like a modern heist plot: fake Juliet's death, break into the family vault with Romeo to retrieve her, and help her disappear before anyone realises anything is amiss. Granted, the Friar is improvising under pressure, but his theatrical solution is highly fraught. Despite his conviction, the plan's dependency on the right people being in the right places at the right moments is distinctly foreboding: there are so many ways this faked death could go wrong.

Q Why might Juliet be willing to trust in the Friar's risky plan?

4.2 Summary: *Wedding preparations are underway. Juliet returns home to ask her father's forgiveness and agree to the impending marriage, much to his delight.*

Once again Juliet tells no lies, but her words are loaded with ambiguity. She tells her father what he wants to hear, to alleviate suspicion and give herself time and space to enact the Friar's plan. There is also the possibility she offers a genuine apology for what she is about to do, and for not being the submissive daughter he wants. She says truthfully that the Friar told her to beg her father's pardon – and when she asks forgiveness and promises to be 'ruled by you' (4.2.21) henceforth, Lord Capulet presumes she is speaking to him. This may be so; however, Juliet could be secretly asking pardon of the Friar for manipulating him, Romeo for her 'agreement' to marry Paris, or – perhaps most convincingly, as she is kneeling in subjugation – she may be asking forgiveness from God.

Key point

Unfortunately, Capulet is so pleased with his daughter's compliance he hastens the wedding date. Timing is critical for success in the Friar's plan. Suddenly everything must happen more quickly and sooner, and the audience's sense of trepidation increases over the problems sure to arise.

Q What competing emotions is each of the main characters experiencing?

4.3 Summary: *Juliet requests to be left alone the night before her wedding and considers all the implications of what may happen if she takes the Friar's potion. The thought of Romeo in danger finally resolves her, and she drinks.*

This night marks the culmination of Juliet's isolation, as she sends away both the Nurse and her mother – the only characters to whom she could turn for advice or support: 'My dismal scene I needs must act alone' (4.3.19). The rest of the scene is her monologue as she wrestles with the enormity of what she is about to do. Her characteristic rationality manifests as she argues with herself about the pros and cons of committing to the plan. If the potion proves ineffective, she has a knife ready for suicide. She worries the Friar has betrayed her – that his potion will kill her to prevent her marriage to Romeo being discovered – but justifies him as 'a holy man' (4.3.29) and trustworthy.

Her musings then change tone, with nightmarish imaginings of being buried alive, going mad or being haunted by ghosts. Juliet has contemplated death before, but her fears of losing hope, her mind or Romeo to a vengeful ghostly Tybalt are what finally compel her to drink. She will face her deepest fears for a chance to be reunited with her husband.

Q Why does Juliet describe her 'state' as being 'cross and full of sin' (4.3.4–5)?

4.4 Summary: *Early in the morning, the Capulet household is busy organising wedding food and entertainment.*

After the dramatic scene of Juliet risking her life, the audience's anticipation and anxieties for her are heightened by this glimpse of chaotic wedding preparations downstairs. This juxtaposition of impending tragedy and unexpected comedy also gives more insight into the household, with stern Lord Capulet now so flighty with delight at the upcoming nuptials he disrupts the domestic order of women and servants at work. He is not even upset when the Nurse chides him for his behaviour, or when his wife comments on his philandering ways.

Q What is revealed about the hierarchy of power in the Capulet household?

4.5 Summary: *The Nurse goes to wake Juliet on her wedding morning, and calls in horror for Lord and Lady Capulet. Juliet's parents, fiancé and companion all express their grief over finding her lifeless, while the Friar attempts to console them. The wedding entertainers are left squabbling about their new role as funeral musicians.*

The audience experiences unresolved tension throughout this scene: either the plan has worked but may be undone at any moment if the faked death is revealed, or the Friar's play-acting is unknowingly ironic, because Juliet is actually dead. The grieving of the other characters has greater complexity in the light of this ambiguity – if we believe the death false, the professions of anguish feel more performative and self-centred, whereas if Juliet has died, it is easier to evoke sympathy and understanding for these characters. This sense of unease is heightened in the strange encounter between Capulet servant Peter and the Musicians. Their self-centred responses further highlight the ambiguities in the Capulet family's reactions.

Key vocabulary

aqua-vitae: a drink containing alcohol.

corse: corpse.

tane: taken.

Q How do each of the characters express their grief?

Act 5

5.1 Summary: *In Mantua, Romeo has been dreaming of Juliet, but his servant brings news of her 'death' and he immediately makes plans to return to Verona. First, though, he forces a poor apothecary to sell him poison, so he can reunite with Juliet in her tomb.*

Romeo's optimistic soliloquy after dreams of Juliet is brutally juxtaposed with the announcement of her death. The audience realises the plan has continued and she has been interred, but are still unsure whether the potion has worked as it should and why there is no letter from the Friar. Balthazar's touching concern for his master will be evident again later: Romeo inspires affection and loyalty from his companions, and is also careful here to protect his servant from culpability.

However, Romeo is devastatingly quick to take action, setting the violent pace for the rest of the Act. Bullying the impoverished Apothecary into selling him illegal poison speaks to his desperation not to live without Juliet, but also reinforces his youth, wealth and unconscious social privilege. He is reckless because he can afford to be, and thinks life holds no worth if spent in suffering and loss. The Apothecary is experienced enough to have learned to value life over death: it is ironic the catalyst for the success of Romeo's sudden plan should be in his hands.

Q Why does Romeo talk so much about the Apothecary – and not about Juliet?

5.2 Summary: *The Friar's plan continues to go wrong – his friend who was to inform Romeo of Juliet's faked death never delivered the message. The Friar hurries to the tomb to help Juliet escape.*

The series of terrible misfortunes continues, and Friar Lawrence's hopeful greeting turns to horror with his friend's apology for not delivering the letter to Romeo. The audience recognises the dramatic irony that misunderstandings and plagues on houses should continue to lead to devastating outcomes throughout this play, but the scene finishes on a hopeful note: both key players in the plan are now heading towards the tomb to rescue Juliet. If only the timing is right, all may yet be well.

Q What is Friar John's reason for not delivering the letter, and what other ideas in the play does it connect with?

5.3 Summary: *Paris keeps vigil at the tomb, and is killed in a fight with Romeo. Seeing Juliet lifeless, Romeo drinks his poison and dies – just as Friar Lawrence arrives. Juliet awakens and the Friar pleads with her to leave, but she refuses and kills herself with a dagger. Local authorities arrive, followed by the Prince, the Capulets and Lord Montague – alone, as his wife has died of grief. The Friar explains what happened, and the families vow to raise statues in honour of their dead children. The Prince speaks final words of mourning for Juliet and Romeo.*

Romeo's desperate pleas to avoid fighting Paris echo the earlier confrontation with Tybalt, as Romeo becomes twice a murderer and both his victims end up in the same tomb. His characteristically emotional speech exacerbates the dramatic tension: Juliet was pale when first discovered 'dead' but, Romeo now notes, is 'crimson in [her] lips and in [her] cheeks' (5.3.95). Only the audience and the Friar know that Juliet is about to wake, but tragically the Friar is too slow, Romeo's speech is not long enough and the 'drugs are quick' (5.3.120).

Once more Romeo's impetuous actions have left Juliet to make a devastating decision. Despite the Friar's entreaty to leave, she chooses to die. Her position as a young noblewoman has meant being deprived of a chance to speak. There is tragic irony in her having to cut her final speech short because, yet again, others are descending to take away her agency – 'Then I'll be brief' (5.3.169).

The play's final moments take an unexpected turn into a police procedural – local law-keepers are dispatched to look for clues, apprehend suspects and call for backup. Eyewitness accounts, objects of interest and confessions reveal the crimes that have taken place, the solution to the mystery of Juliet 'dying' twice, and how extra corpses turned up in her tomb.

Key point

The feud appears to be resolved – Capulet and Montague accept joint responsibility for the tragedy, shake hands in mourning and promise to honour the other's child. However, as the two patriarchs discuss erecting statues for their children, are they truly acting in a spirit of reconciliation, or are they trying to outdo each other and vie for control? Perhaps these two families have learned nothing from this tragedy after all. Yet the play's final lines, spoken by the Prince and serving as an epilogue, promise justice and 'more talk of these sad things' (5.3.307), so there is hope that the import of the story of 'Juliet and her Romeo' (5.3.310) will not be forgotten.

Q Why might the final scene continue on so long after the tragic climax?

CHARACTERS & RELATIONSHIPS

THE HOUSE OF CAPULET

Juliet

Key quotes

'What's in a name? That which we call a rose
By any other word would smell as sweet ...' (2.2.43–4)

'My bounty is as boundless as the sea,
My love as deep; the more I give to thee
The more I have, for both are infinite.' (2.2.133–5)

'Love give me strength, and strength shall help afford.' (4.1.125)

The only child of the wealthy and powerful Lord Capulet, Juliet has grown up burdened with expectations of social and familial duty. Although only thirteen, she is expected to undergo an arranged marriage to secure the family's social standing, and afterwards to continue the family lineage by providing heirs.

As a young noblewoman in Renaissance Verona, Juliet has led a highly sheltered life. However, despite her age and upbringing, she is presented as mature, intelligent and resourceful. In falling in love with the son of her family's rivals, Juliet must choose between fulfilling the obligations of her role as daughter and Capulet heir, and pursuing her own desires. Her growing independence throughout the play indicates her maturity – or perhaps her impetuousness, depending on how her decisions from the point of Romeo's banishment are interpreted.

Key point

Juliet often sees straight to the core of complex issues – in evaluating the worth of a name, she immediately understands the complications of beginning a relationship with Romeo, and recognises that neither he nor she should be defined by family names or feuds. Her discernment, however, is at odds with her youthful infatuation. She pleads with Romeo to stay after their wedding night, although she knows he would be risking his life, and later debates with herself about the perils of taking the Friar's potion before suddenly choosing to consume it.

Lord Capulet

Key quotes

'But Montague is bound as well as I,
In penalty alike, and 'tis not hard, I think,
For men so old as we to keep the peace.' (1.2.1–3)

'My will to her consent is but a part;
And she agreed, within her scope of choice
Lies my consent and fair according voice.' (1.2.17–19)

'Speak not, reply not, do not answer me!
My fingers itch.' (3.5.163–4)

Lord Capulet is rife with contradictions. He is protective of his only child, although he shows little sympathy for his wife and may even have been unfaithful to her. He holds strong patriarchal views when it comes to his role as the head of the Capulet household and an established leader in Veronese society, but at his party he allows Romeo to stay, prioritising good manners over the feud with the Montagues. He hesitates when Paris pressures him for Juliet's hand in marriage, due to her age and because he wants her consent, but he eventually succumbs – suggesting his desire to maintain the Capulets' social prestige and lineage ultimately outweighs fatherly love. This is reinforced when his daughter defies his orders and he becomes abusive and threatens violence. His quick shift to giddy delight when he believes he has got his way, his impetuous decision to bring forward the wedding date and the questionable sincerity of his public grief for his daughter's death all cast doubts on his moral worth.

Lady Capulet

Key quotes

'By my count,
I was your mother much upon these years
That you are now a maid.' (1.3.72–4)

'I beg for justice, which thou, Prince, must give:
Romeo slew Tybalt, Romeo must not live.' (3.1.171–2)

In Act 1 Lady Capulet reveals she married young, giving us significant insight into her circumstances. She became a mother around age thirteen; she can therefore only be about twenty-six years old in the play, and likely had a similarly controlled upbringing to Juliet. While we do not know Lord Capulet's age, he admits he is 'past [his] dancing days' (1.5.30) and that the time when he could court a young woman is 'gone' (1.5.23), suggesting he is much older than his wife. From Lady Capulet's perspective, Paris is a young and desirable suitor, plus there will be prestige in a successful union between her only child and a relative of Veronese royalty.

Unlike the Nurse, who raised Juliet and knows her well, Lady Capulet seems distant from her daughter. However, the grief she exhibits at finding her child's lifeless body – and upon realising they buried her alive and have now lost her again – indicates she felt genuine love for Juliet as her 'one thing to rejoice and solace in' (4.5.47) even if she was not practised at expressing her feelings.

Tybalt

Key quotes

'What, drawn and talk of peace? I hate the word,
As I hate hell, all Montagues, and thee.' (1.1.61–2)

'Now by the stock and honour of my kin,
To strike him dead I hold it not a sin.' (1.5.57–8)

The motivations for Tybalt's dedication to upholding the family feud are complex. He is devoted to maintaining the Capulets' reputation, but he also loves violence and any chance to exhibit his fighting prowess, from his initial encounter with Benvolio to his final moments with Romeo. These values are challenged when his uncle prevents him from confronting Romeo at the party – upholding family honour conflicts with his loyalty to the head of the household, and he must curb his violent tendencies. However, this is not enough to prevent him later defying his uncle's order and the Prince's decree, by pursuing Romeo and ultimately killing Mercutio.

Tybalt seems focused on inciting others into conflict, often using inflammatory language, but the women in the Capulet family see his softer side. Upon his death Lady Capulet laments the loss of her 'brother's child' (3.1.137) and begs for justice; the Nurse deems him 'courteous' and an 'honest gentleman' (3.2.61–2), declaring him (perhaps with exaggeration) 'the best friend I had!'; and Juliet names him her 'dearest cousin' (3.2.66). It seems Tybalt behaves very differently with men in the public sphere compared to how he behaves with the women in his life, who genuinely seem to mourn his loss.

The Nurse

Key quotes

'For Juliet's sake, for her sake, rise and stand …' (3.3.89)

'I think you are happy in this second match,
For it excels your first, or if it did not,
Your first is dead, or 'twere as good he were
As living here and you no use of him.' (3.5.222–5)

'O woe! O woeful, woeful, woeful day!' (4.5.49)

The Nurse occupies a unique social role. She was the hired wet nurse (a woman employed to breastfeed and care for a young child) when Juliet was a baby, but has continued on in the household as companion, confidante, chaperone and unofficial member of the Capulet family. Thus, her position transcends her class and gender – she is allowed to get away with indecorous behaviour and vulgar language in front of her employers, as well as have her own servant (or perhaps boyfriend?), Peter.

Although her character is comedic, with her bawdy humour, verbosity and untimely interruptions, the Nurse also displays pathos and nuance. Her own baby died, which helps us understand her devotion to Juliet, her 'ladybird' (1.3.3), in risking her job to facilitate Juliet's marriage to Romeo. However, she also reveals a mercenary attitude in valuing wealth and stability over romance, which she considers fickle, as shown when she recommends Juliet commit bigamy rather than stay devoted to an absent husband. Although she is a surrogate mother to Juliet and displays more affection than Lady Capulet, Juliet views her crudely practical suggestion as a betrayal, and confides in her no further. The Nurse's final appearance in the play reiterates her maternal love: this verbose character is so distressed upon discovering the child she raised apparently dead that she cannot find words to express her grief, and only repeats the same laments over and over.

THE HOUSE OF MONTAGUE

Romeo

Key quotes

'If I profane with my unworthiest hand
This holy shrine, the gentle sin is this,
My lips, two blushing pilgrims, ready stand
To smooth that rough touch with a tender kiss.' (1.5.92–5)

'Do thou but close our hands with holy words,
Then love-devouring Death do what he dare,
It is enough I may but call her mine.' (2.6.6–8)

'... O here
Will I set up my everlasting rest,
And shake the yoke of inauspicious stars
From this world-wearied flesh.' (5.3.109–12)

Initially, Romeo seems to be a familiar depiction of a seventeen-year-old. He likes hanging out and joking with his friends, and agrees to gatecrash a party when opportunity arises. He is often impulsive, he can be reckless, and his parents do not understand him. His recent tendency towards depression, staying out all night and remaining in his darkened room all day, is purportedly because he has a crush on a girl who is not interested in him – Lord Capulet's 'fair niece' (1.2.69) Rosaline.

However, like Juliet, Romeo is subjected to intense familial and social pressure, and we can understand that his emotional irregularity might have additional causes. Lord Capulet says that 'Verona brags of him / To be a virtuous and well-governed youth' (1.5.66–7), but, as the only son of a powerful family, Romeo is also expected to carry on the family name, marry well and sire heirs. His father has no time for his feelings of angst, his male friends have no real sympathy for his sensitivity, and his male peers have no tolerance for his efforts to avoid conflict.

There is an argument to be made for his fickleness and immaturity in immediately discarding Rosaline upon seeing Juliet, but there is also the possibility the connection he makes with the daughter of his family's enemy becomes an opportunity for significant character growth and increasing emotional intelligence.

Key point

Juliet may undermine Romeo's overblown romantic speeches, such as when she interrupts him in 2.2 (e.g. 'O swear not by the moon' 2.2.109), but the sincerity of his love for her overcomes many other influences in his life. However, upon Mercutio's death, anger, guilt and fraternal love provoke Romeo to ruin the chances of his marriage ever effecting an interfamily reconciliation, for it was likely that either he or Tybalt would die in their encounter. Moreover, his impatience to be reunited with Juliet in death not only leads to Paris' death, but also forestalls the possibility of a reunion for the lovers, as, devastatingly, his suicide happens faster than Juliet's revival.

Lord Montague

Key quotes

'Thou villain Capulet! – Hold me not, let me go.' (1.1.70)

'Could we but learn from whence his sorrows grow,
We would as willingly give cure as know.' (1.1.145–6)

'O thou untaught! what manners is in this,
To press before thy father to a grave?' (5.3.214–5)

In Scene 1, like his rival, Lord Capulet, Lord Montague is incensed by encountering his enemy, but asks later, 'Who set this ancient quarrel new abroach?' (1.1.95). As a father, he seems more concerned with the future of his only son than with Veronese politics, but he demonstrates limited sympathy towards Romeo, considering his depression 'black and portentous' (1.1.132). It is notable that Romeo turns to Friar Lawrence, rather than his father, for counsel and support in times of trouble. Lord Montague's brief mention of his wife's death, complaint of Romeo's impropriety on learning of his fate, and apparent effort to outdo Lord Capulet's offer of reconciliation with a display of wealth and power, may suggest a man who struggles with emotional intelligence and remains more concerned with appearance than with family.

Lady Montague

Key quotes

'Thou shalt not stir one foot to seek a foe.' (1.1.71)

'O where is Romeo? saw you him today?
Right glad I am he was not at this fray.' (1.1.107–8)

Despite being married to the head of the powerful Montague family, Romeo's mother is barely seen or heard in the play. She worries significantly about her family, however – in the opening scene she tries to prevent her husband from fighting and is relieved Romeo is not involved in the feud. This emotional burden proves the source of her unexpected offstage death from grief at Romeo's exile, which, like her life, is overshadowed by other characters and events.

Benvolio

Key quotes

'I do but keep the peace. Put up thy sword,
Or manage it to part these men with me.' (1.1.59–60)

'Stand not amazed, the Prince will doom thee death
If thou art taken. Hence be gone, away!' (3.1.125–6)

'Benvolio' means 'benevolent' or 'peacekeeper' in Italian and, as his name suggests, Benvolio arrives in the play as a voice of sense and reason. He intervenes in the opening street fight to restore the peace, pleading with Tybalt to behave like a gentleman in public despite their families' conflict. Lord Montague entrusts him with discovering the cause of Romeo's depression, and Romeo in turn trusts his cousin enough to confess his unrequited love. Benvolio is also a calming influence on the rambunctious Mercutio, endeavouring to prevent him causing too much mischief and to curb his more offensive remarks. Benvolio's final appearance in the play parallels his first – once again he is embroiled in a violent encounter arising from the feud, but this time he does not intervene in the fight, and in this final appearance, he does not prevent Mercutio from taking up the challenge on Romeo's behalf. He is curiously silent throughout this scene (which opens up new possibilities for interpreting his motivations and character), until the moment of crisis, whereupon he steps up to try to help his friends. Mercutio dies offstage in his arms, then Benvolio risks death by telling Romeo to flee, while staying himself, hoping that his exposition will be convincing enough to spare his own life and moderate the irate Prince's punishment of his surviving friend.

OTHER CHARACTERS

Prince Escales

Key quotes

'... What ho, you men, you beasts!
That quench the fire of your pernicious rage
With purple fountains issuing from your veins:
On pain of torture, from those bloody hands
Throw your mistempered weapons to the ground ...' (1.1.74–8)

'And I for winking at your discords too
Have lost a brace of kinsmen. All are punished.' (5.3.294–5)

'Go hence to have more talk of these sad things;
Some shall be pardoned, and some punishèd:
For never was a story of more woe
Than this of Juliet and her Romeo.' (5.3.307–10)

As ruler of Verona, the Prince has no private life in the play: every appearance is public, politicised and performative. Nonetheless, his incisive, eloquent speeches show an erudite, well-intentioned man, quick to act, but who also endeavours to be fair. After the opening fight, the Prince's threats of punishment prove ineffectual. Yet his efficiency at evaluating a situation is evident when investigating the deaths of Tybalt and Mercutio, and when examining witnesses and evidence to discover the truth at the play's denouement. The Prince also values justice: he claims, 'Mercy but murders, pardoning those that kill' (3.1.188), although he chooses to exile Romeo rather than execute him, and he promises consequences for those involved after the lovers' deaths, although we can only speculate on what that might mean.

Perhaps the most admirable trait Prince Escales displays is humility. He admits he failed in his duty as leader by not resolving the feud before it turned tragic, and openly blames himself for the deaths of his family members Mercutio and Paris – but he is adept at influencing audiences with fine speeches, and we may question to what extent he exerts those skills on us, too.

Mercutio

Key quotes

'If love be rough with you, be rough with love:
Prick love for pricking, and you beat love down.' (1.4.27–8)

'Men's eyes were made to look, and let them gaze;
I will not budge for no man's pleasure, I.' (3.1.47–8)

'Ask for me tomorrow, and you shall find me a grave man.' (3.1.89–90)

Mercutio is a kinsman of the Prince, and therefore should be impartial in the feud. However, his two best friends are Montagues, and Mercutio determines his fealty is to them and the Montague clan when it becomes a matter of life and death. Mercutio is beloved by critics and audiences alike for his wit and daring, but also because of his loyalty to and love for his friends.

This is evident when, amid comic banter, Mercutio worries about Romeo's safety: 'is he a man to encounter Tybalt?' (2.4.15–16). When he later accuses his friend of 'calm, dishonourable, vile submission' (3.1.66) and thus fatally takes Romeo's place in the duel, we speculate about his motivations. It would not be out of character for Mercutio to be genuinely incensed by Romeo's pacifism – despite his political neutrality, he has thrown in his lot with the Montagues and is willing to fight in their name. Moreover, he has proven his contempt for romantic love or delicate emotion, so it is plausible he is repulsed by what he perceives as Romeo's emasculated response and feels compelled to 'man up' on his behalf. However, Mercutio also coaxes Romeo out of stagnating depression and to a party, stays out late looking for him afterwards (despite complaining) and affectionately trades insults with him. It is not unreasonable to suspect he deliberately engages Tybalt in order to save his friend's life. No wonder, then, that he is indignant when Romeo intervenes – which he implies was the cause of his fatal injury. Yet even in dying, Mercutio cannot be 'grave' (3.1.90), and exclaims, complains and cracks jokes until his unexpectedly tragi-comic end.

Paris

Key quotes

'Immoderately she weeps for Tybalt's death,
And therefore have I little talked of love …' (4.1.6–7)

'Condemnèd villain, I do apprehend thee.
Obey and go with me, for thou must die.' (5.3.56–7)

Paris is of central importance to the plot, as his proposal becomes both an impediment to Romeo and Juliet and the instigator of key actions, but his character and values are difficult to discern. He is frequently praised for his looks and charm, but as he is near-royalty and therefore an influential man in Verona, this may be mere flattery from others. His conversations with Lord Capulet about marrying Juliet are brief and businesslike in tone: aligning with a wealthy and well-reputed family by marrying their only daughter may matter to Paris more than his bride does, and explain why he is eager to hurry the wedding despite Juliet's age.

Later in the play Paris does appear attentive to his fiancée, but his concern is marred by his sense of ownership over her: 'Thy face is mine' (4.1.35). His death scene is also ambiguous: it seems both noble and foolish to provoke a fight with a known murderer over suspicion of vandalism. Moreover, he 'would not be seen' (5.3.2) weeping at Juliet's grave, so when Romeo describes him by saying 'One writ with me in sour misfortune's book!' (5.3.82) and carries him into the tomb for an honourable burial, he may be acknowledging their shared tragedy as sensitive men unable to survive an intolerant society.

Friar Lawrence

Key quotes

'In one respect I'll thy assistant be:
For this alliance may so happy prove
To turn your households' rancour to pure love.' (2.3.90–2)

'And if thou dar'st, I'll give thee remedy.' (4.1.76)

'... if ought in this
Miscarried by my fault, let my old life
Be sacrificed, some hour before his time,
Unto the rigour of severest law.' (5.3.266–9)

As a man of peace caught up in the conflict, the Friar is in a difficult position politically and personally. He is the trusted family friend of and priest to both feuding households, the authority on morality and God, and the conductor of weddings and funerals. His skills in deception have an immense impact on the play's outcome.

When Romeo comes to him for help, Friar Lawrence's reaction is both professional and paternal. He knows this 'son' and his secrets far better than Romeo's own father does; however, he has a duty to promote peace in God's name. There is also self-interest and political angling in agreeing to marry Romeo and Juliet to broker reconciliation between their families. Similar tensions inform his later actions. He is distressed by Juliet's threat of self-harm, and thus concocts the dramatic plan and remarkable potion to solve her dilemma. However, his job and mortal soul are also endangered – if he marries Juliet to Paris, he is condoning bigamy and will thus be ruined in the sight of God, and in the view of society if it was ever revealed.

Juliet worries the Friar may betray her but concludes he is 'a holy man' (4.3.29). When she will not leave Romeo's side after his death, the Friar does flee in fear, but his efforts throughout the play to help the lovers, right his wrongs (however unsuccessfully) and finally reveal all – even if it means his death – suggest Juliet's judgement is sound.

THEMES, IDEAS & VALUES

Love and duty

Key quotes

'Here's much to do with hate, but more with love:
Why then, O brawling love, O loving hate,
O any thing of nothing first create!' (Romeo, 1.1.166–8)

'My only love sprung from my only hate!
Too early seen unknown, and known too late!
Prodigious birth of love it is to me,
That I must love a loathèd enemy.' (Juliet, 1.5.137–40)

Romeo and Juliet is famous as a love story, but the Prologue reveals this is a play about conflicts between love and duty. When each title character discovers the identity of their new love interest, they are torn between developing romantic feelings, and loyalty to their family in spurning an enemy. This tension informs their decisions in the play.

Before they even meet, both Romeo and Juliet have observed the decisions others make between love and duty: Romeo recognises the ongoing feud is more about love for family than hatred and violence, while Juliet sees the irony that she should fall in love with an enemy she is meant to hate but has only just met. It is telling we never learn what started the antagonism between the Capulets and Montagues.

Other forms of love and duty also inform the play. Lord Capulet considers Juliet undutiful and unloving because she will not obey his edict to marry Paris, while the Nurse helps Juliet marry Romeo despite her loyalty to her employers. Mercutio prioritises duty above love, listing concepts of love and reasons to be sceptical of them in his Queen Mab monologue (1.4.53–95).

There are many more ways the tension between love and duty play out within the text. For example:

- love for family and friends, including between the lovers, but also shown in Benvolio and Mercutio's affection for Romeo

- desire for honour or power, exemplified in Tybalt, but affecting Paris, Capulet and Montague as well
- passion for violence, sex or mischief, as seen with the Nurse or Mercutio
- self-love and self-worth, as with Juliet, her father and Rosaline
- love for tradition and rules, such as Capulet's edict about Juliet's marriage or the Prince's commands
- desire for independence in love, as professed by both Romeo and Juliet
- duty to moral or social codes of conduct, which trouble the Friar and the Prince
- loyalty to allies, as between Mercutio, Benvolio and Romeo
- duty to honour a spouse's desires above one's own, demonstrated by Juliet and her mother
- loyalty to one's profession or social position, shown by the Prince, various household servants and the Apothecary
- loyalty shown by risking death to physically or verbally defend others or proclaim one's loyalty, as Tybalt and Mercutio do.

Destiny and free will

Key quotes

'I fear too early, for my mind misgives
Some consequence yet hanging in the stars …
But He that hath the steerage of my course
Direct my sail!' (Romeo, 1.4.106–07, 112–13)

'O Fortune, Fortune, all men call thee fickle;
If thou art fickle, what dost thou with him
That is renowned for faith?' (Juliet, 3.5.60–2)

The question of whether humans have control over their own existence is a central concern in *Romeo and Juliet*. In the Elizabethan world, God was considered the ultimate authority over human existence, but the Church acknowledged the problematic relationship between faith and free will. If God rules all and decides all, then the future is already set, so our actions and choices are irrelevant. However, if we have free will, we can make moral and ethical decisions for ourselves in God's name. The Prologue refers to 'star-crossed lovers' (line 6), and there are multiple references to the characters' destinies being written in the stars, and therefore fixed. However, it is not made clear exactly what is determined by fate. Were the lovers only fated to meet? Fated to marry? Were they always destined to die? Romeo rails against this notion of fate upon hearing of Juliet's apparent death – 'I defy you, stars!' (5.1.24) – but his plan is suicide. Perhaps he believed his fate was never to be with Juliet in life, so he attempts to be with her in death at least.

However, it is Romeo's choice to kill himself that sparks Juliet's own decision to die. If he had chosen to wait for the Friar's message, stay in Mantua and grieve – or even if he had acted less rashly upon discovering his wife in the Capulet tomb – he and Juliet could have been reunited.

Thus, there are numerous points in the play where it seems the outcome depends entirely on one individual's decision, or where a character choosing to act either sooner or less impulsively would have dramatically altered the consequent series of events.

Key point

The phrase 'star-crossed lovers' (Prologue, line 6) suggests that, as the stars were not aligned for Romeo and Juliet, they were destined for misfortune. However, this metaphor also evokes imagery of bright, luminous objects accidently crossing paths – a lucky happenstance, or dangerous and destructive?

Social rules and conflict

Key quotes

'From ancient grudge break to new mutiny,
Where civil blood makes civil hands unclean.' (Chorus, Prologue, lines 3–4)

'These violent delights have violent ends,
And in their triumph die like fire and powder,
Which as they kiss consume.' (Friar Lawrence, 2.6.9–11)

'Some shall be pardoned, and some punishèd.' (The Prince, 5.3.308)

Verona is governed by strict rules of conduct, religion and class, but these rules are undermined or broken throughout the play. Some of these rules are systemic: the Prince's decrees represent the rule of law, and the need for the Friar's blessing of a marriage represents the authority of the Church. However, others reflect the values of Veronese high society, such as patriarchal enforcement of gender roles, seniority dictating family leadership, and unspoken rules about etiquette or social niceties.

There is a conflict within the play about conflict – the Friar warns that violent passions will end violently, and the rebellion that many characters demonstrate against royal decrees, patriarchal power and social expectations all lead to tragedy. However, it is implied at several points in the play that there is a need to break rules or defy authority when it is unfeeling, unjust or ignorant, as when the Friar and the Nurse both risk supporting the lovers, Lady Capulet and Lady Montague chastise their foolish husbands, or Juliet defies her father. Significant problems are therefore created or exacerbated by characters determined to reinforce the systems or values regulating this society and by those struggling to redefine them.

Adolescence and family dynamics

Key quotes

'Could we but learn from whence his sorrows grow,
We would as willingly give cure as know.' (Lord Montague about Romeo, 1.1.145–6)

'Hang thee, young baggage, disobedient wretch!
I tell thee what: get thee to church a 'Thursday,
Or never after look me in the face.' (Lord Capulet to Juliet, 3.5.160–2)

'Talk not to me, for I'll not speak a word.
Do as thou wilt, for I have done with thee.' (Lady Capulet to Juliet, 3.5.202–3)

Shakespeare's Elizabethan audience did not have a concept of 'teenagers', or even a clear distinction between children and adults. Yet this play chimes strongly with modern audiences due to its depiction of the adolescent experience. From dealing with pressure from parents and peers, trying to 'fit in' with family or community, developing crushes and exploring sexuality, crashing parties and playing pranks, to coping with issues of puberty, mental health and self-identity, we empathise with the play's younger characters because of our own experiences growing up, despite the centuries separating us from this world.

We also witness characters struggling with the pressures of other familial roles, and see different depictions of fatherhood, motherhood, fraternity, marriage and legacy in Verona. Consider the Friar as a 'holy father' (4.1.37) and the Nurse as a surrogate mother, and their efforts to reconcile parental urges with their more official social or professional obligations. Moreover, Tybalt's extreme loyalty, as heir to the family feud, costs him his life, while Romeo's actions test his honorary brotherhood with Benvolio and Mercutio. The Capulets' marital problems form an interesting counterpoint to the pressure they exert on their daughter to marry Paris, and then we must witness the destruction of family lineage when they lose Juliet, while Lord Montague loses both wife and son, and thus all hope of descendants and the continuation of the family name. Family is demonstrated to be a powerful and persuasive force for the key characters, and part of the play's tragedy is that the various desires to strengthen family ties or forge new familial alliances for marriage, children and love lead to lost relationships and loved ones.

Gender roles

Key quotes

'And all my fortunes at thy foot I'll lay,
And follow thee my lord throughout the world.' (Juliet, 2.2.147–8)

'Thy beauty hath made me effeminate,
And in my temper softened valour's steel!' (Romeo about Juliet, 3.1.105–6)

'And this shall free thee from this present shame,
If no inconstant toy, nor womanish fear,
Abate thy valour in the acting it.' (Friar Lawrence, 4.1.118–20)

Verona's strict patriarchal system is problematic for both sexes in the play. In *Romeo and Juliet,* an individual's agency, relationships, ability to express opinions and emotions, and other social behaviours are all dictated by one's gender, so gender expectations and pressures to conform to them cause significant issues for multiple characters. Romeo does not adhere to his society's expectations of a man: he is sensitive, emotional and deliberately avoids conflict. He would rather speak of love in sonnets than have coarse conversations about sex, and he values Juliet as an equal. As a result, his friends tease him for his delicate nature, his father is unable to understand his depression, and even his mentor, Friar Lawrence, berates his tears – upon having committed a murder, no less – as 'womanish' (3.3.110).

However, while Romeo can stay out all night and meet up with friends whenever he likes, Juliet's movements are constrained. The play depicts the relative freedom young noblemen of Verona experience: Romeo, Mercutio, Benvolio, Tybalt and Paris can go anywhere and do and say almost anything they please. Other than Rosaline, who is never seen, Juliet is the only young woman in the play, which emphasises her isolation within this world. Church, family and society all deem her an asset of her father's, to be married off. Juliet challenges traditional female expectations by wanting a husband on her own terms. She kisses a stranger, gets married in secret, refuses an arranged marriage and plans to flee with her new husband to start a new life, all actions considered sinful for a noblewoman in Verona. However, she is unable to execute this plan, and we can question whether she is able to overcome patriarchal pressures or whether she ultimately succumbs to them.

Other characters also bear the burden of gender expectations. Although the Nurse is an older, worldly woman, she still must have Peter as chaperone, and is mocked by Mercutio in the streets. In response, she is willing to 'take him down' (2.4.125) – although it is unclear whether she means physically, verbally or sexually. Lady Capulet has had to deal with her husband's philandering, while Lady Montague rarely has an opportunity to say a word. Even the esteemed Count Paris has his servant keep a lookout so that no one sees him crying at his fiancée's grave.

Key point

Male culture in Verona is characterised by aggression and the objectification of women. This emerges as a key reason for many conflicts within the play.

Identity and personal growth

Key quotes

'O swear not by the moon, th'inconstant moon,
That monthly changes in her circled orb,
Lest that thy love prove likewise variable.' (Juliet to Romeo, 2.2.109–11)

'I have no joy of this contract tonight,
It is too rash, too unadvised, too sudden,
Too like the lightning, which doth cease to be
Ere one can say "It lightens". Sweet, good night:
This bud of love, by summer's ripening breath,
May prove a beauteous flower when next we meet.'
(Juliet to Romeo, 2.2.117–22)

Juliet's metaphors of love as changeable as the moon, sudden as lighting or blossoming like a flower invite considerations of how the lovers might develop or mature over the course of their brief relationship. Both Romeo and Juliet struggle to embrace their roles in this world, including the expectations of gender, family obligation, social duty and religious morality. They also both question the significance of their names. Different performances and scholarly critiques of the play have interpreted their actions in different ways: is Romeo's downfall due in part to childishness and spontaneity, or are his attempts to avoid fights with Tybalt and Paris, and his final resolution to join his wife in death, evidence of his emotional growth and maturity? Juliet values rational thinking and circumspection, but makes many rash decisions throughout the play – should we understand this as an indication of her youth and immaturity, or do we see her evolution into independence as she progresses from silent and obedient to vocal and defiant?

This theme resonates with other characters in the play, including the Prince, struggling with his role as arbitrator; Lord Capulet, trying to cling onto his patriarchal power when it is challenged; and Paris, who is unexpectedly willing to defend his fiancée's tomb with his life. We can also ask whether characters such as Mercutio or Tybalt develop in any significant way: one dies making jokes and the other shouting threats.

Light and darkness

Key quotes

'But soft, what light through yonder window breaks?
It is the east, and Juliet is the sun.
Arise, fair sun, and kill the envious moon ...' (Romeo, 2.2.2–4)

'Come, Night, come, Romeo, come, thou day in night,
For thou wilt lie upon the wings of night,
Whiter than new snow upon a raven's back.' (Juliet, 3.2.17–19)

'More light and light, more dark and dark our woes!' (Romeo, 3.5.36)

In a play of complex dichotomies (opposites), the motif of light and its relationship with darkness has significant meaning. Both lovers refer to each other's presence as daylight in the night, evoking connotations of love as enlightening and illuminating, surrounded by the threat of a dark world. However, darkness also allows for privacy, as when Romeo is mourning his unrequited love for Rosaline, and when Juliet is excited for her wedding night. After Tybalt's murder, dawning day represents danger, and only serves to darken the couple's future.

The nuanced interplay between darkness and light throughout the play also pervades plot and setting, as key events are impacted by nightfall or dawn. The Prince observes the sunless morning of the lovers' death, implying that their youth and promise is a light that has been extinguished.

Sickness and health

Key quotes

'Within the infant rind of this weak flower
Poison hath residence, and medicine power:
For this, being smelt, with that part cheers each part,
Being tasted, stays all senses with the heart.' (Friar Lawrence, 2.3.23–6)

'I am hurt.
A plague a'both houses! I am sped.' (Mercutio, 3.1.82–3)

'There is thy gold, worse poison to men's souls,
Doing more murder in this loathsome world,
Than these poor compounds that thou mayst not sell.' (Romeo, 5.1.80–2)

In a tragedy concerned with life and death, states of sickness and health are crucial to the plot. The Friar's sleeping potion, Romeo's fatal poison and poor Friar John's quarantine all have tremendous consequences.

Metaphors of infection, healing and restoration are also a common motif in the play to describe strong emotions and social disorder. Both Romeo and Benvolio talk of love as a sickness, and the Prince accuses Capulet and Montague of having 'cankered hate' (1.1.86). Mercutio's thrice-uttered curse as he is dying – 'A plague a'both your houses!' (3.1.97) – becomes a threat and a prophecy, recognising the family feud as a disease on society that has killed him and will render them barren.

As a herbalist, Friar Lawrence muses on how a tiny plant can have the capacity to kill or to cure, and how that is like the capacity for good and evil in people. The question of whether all will ever be well in Verona, and if such metaphoric diseases can actually be healed, lingers at the end of the play.

Miscommunication

Key quotes

'Her body sleeps in the Capels' monument ...
I saw her laid low in her kindred's vault,
And presently took post to tell it you.' (Balthasar, 5.1.18, 20–1)

'Unhappy fortune! By my brotherhood,
The letter was not nice but full of charge,
Of dear import, and the neglecting it
May do much danger.' (Friar Lawrence, 5.2.17–20)

At multiple points in the play, communications between characters break down. Lord Montague cannot ascertain from his son what troubles him; Romeo cannot confess to his friends that he has secretly married or explain to Tybalt why he does not want to fight. Juliet is rarely offered the chance to voice an opinion in early scenes, is shouted down by her father when she tries to speak up for herself, and stops confessing to the Nurse when she encourages her to marry Paris. The Prince makes authoritative speeches, but his decrees are ignored as the 'ancient grudge' (Prologue, line 3) continues.

Numerous misunderstandings also occur throughout the play. Benvolio thinks Romeo's problem is that he is still in love with Rosaline. Lord Capulet presumes Juliet is sad over Tybalt's death and will be cheered by marrying Paris. Paris is convinced the only reason Romeo would be at Juliet's tomb would be to defile it. We never even learn what the Capulets and Montagues were feuding about in the first place – the origins of the conflict have been lost to history.

Finally, when key messages are compromised, there is a significant impact on the plot. Capulet's private party is crashed because his messenger was unable to read the invitations himself, while Friar Lawrence's friend is quarantined and cannot deliver the vital message to Romeo in Mantua, that Juliet is only faking her death.

The freedom to state an opinion, share feelings openly or ask others to explain their meaning is shown to be limited in this society. Characters must conceal their desires and curtail their words for their safety, out of concern for others or due to the vulnerability of their social position.

Time

Key quotes

'From ancient grudge break to new mutiny …' (Chorus, Prologue, line 3)

'Wisely and slow, they stumble that run fast.' (Friar Lawrence, 2.3.94)

'I must hear from thee every day in the hour,
For in a minute there are many days.
O, by this count I shall be much in years
Ere I again behold my Romeo!' (Juliet, 3.5.44–7)

With so much happening so quickly in this play, it is easy to lose sight of the actual time line. The narrative takes place over a mere five days. Juliet and Romeo meet at the party on Sunday night and marry the very next day, and Romeo kills Tybalt just afterwards. The lovers spend Monday night together and Romeo flees on Tuesday, whereupon Juliet is told her marriage to Paris is set for Thursday. She plots with the Friar and 'agrees' to the marriage on Tuesday night – only for her father to change the wedding to Wednesday. So Juliet fakes her death immediately, her body is discovered on Wednesday, and Romeo gets the news of her death on Thursday. He arrives at her tomb that evening, and their deaths occur before the sun rises on Friday morning.

The pace and urgency of events is contrasted with the Friar's regular admonishments to pause and take time to make careful, well-considered decisions – although he himself fails to do this when pressured by both Romeo and Juliet for help. This theme of risky, hasty, impetuous behaviour versus calm, rational, prolonged planning is explored through several characters. The audience sees the contrast between Benvolio pleading for Tybalt to wait before fighting, Romeo being chided by Juliet for declaring love so quickly, and Lady Capulet and Lady Montague advising their husbands to wait a moment before doing something reckless.

Other concerns in the play about the importance of time include:

- the significance of history and remembering the past versus the vitality of the present and the need to focus on what is happening right now
- the value of considering the consequences before acting
- contrasts between youth and age
- contrasts between what is fleeting and what is immortal
- the conflict between traditional values and new ways of thinking and behaving.

DIFFERENT INTERPRETATIONS

Different interpretations arise from different responses to a text. Over time, a text will evoke a wide range of responses from its readers, who may come from various social or cultural groups and live in very different places and historical periods. Responses by critics and reviewers can be published in newspapers, journals and books, both online and in print. They can also be expressed in discussions among readers in the media, classrooms, book groups and so on.

While there is no single correct reading or interpretation of a text, it is important to understand that an interpretation is more than a personal opinion – it is the justification of a point of view on the text. To present an interpretation of a text based on your point of view, you must use a logical argument and support it with relevant evidence from the text.

Critical viewpoints

Romeo and Juliet, one of Shakespeare's most famous and beloved plays, has sparked an extraordinary amount of scholarship. Books, articles, essays, documentaries, new productions and performances, reimaginings and reworkings: viewpoints on approaching and understanding this text are diverse.

Esteemed Shakespearean critic Harold Bloom championed reading literary classics for their aesthetic and linguistic value rather than through political or sociological lenses, so had no patience for feminist, class-based or postcolonial readings of Shakespeare. He believed a key achievement in Shakespeare's work was the notion of characters with complex and evolving personalities. In his famous book on this theory, *Shakespeare: The Invention of the Human*, Bloom argues that '*Romeo and Juliet* matters' because of 'four exuberantly realized characters' (Bloom 1999, p.89): Romeo, Juliet, Mercutio and the Nurse. Dubbing

Mercutio 'the scene stealer of the play', he suggests that Romeo's friend had to be killed so as not to distract the audience from the 'erotic greatness of Juliet' and the 'heroic effort of Romeo to approximate her sublime state of being in love' (p.89). To Bloom, the play is 'the largest and most persuasive celebration of romantic love in Western literature' (p.90), and the 'absurd pathos' of the ending, with wretched characters attempting reconciliation and understanding, leaves the audience to speculate 'to what degree its young lovers are responsible for their own catastrophe' (p.103).

Bloom expanded upon these notions in a later essay, calling the play 'a vision of an uncompromising love that perishes of its own idealism and intensity', and claiming:

> ... Romeo, exalted by the authentic love between the even more vital Juliet and him, is one of the first instances of the Shakespearean representation of crucial change in a character through self-overhearing and self-reflection. Juliet, an even larger instance, is the play's triumph, since she inaugurates Shakespeare's extraordinary procession of vibrant, life-enhancing women, never matched before or since in all of Western literature ... (Bloom 2010, p.7)

Thus though both their deaths are 'tragic', 'Juliet ... transcends her self-destruction and dies exalted. Romeo, not of her eminence, dies more pathetically ... Shakespeare sees to it that our larger loss is the loss of Juliet' (p.9). Bloom's interpretation focuses on Juliet as the emotional centre of the play and the catalyst for Romeo's evolution as a character, and believes the lovers' inability to compromise their idealism leads to the tragedy.

Acclaimed Shakespearean academic Marjorie Garber agrees that the 'most striking instance of [character] growth in the play is the transformation that Juliet undergoes' (Garber 2004, p.205), and considers how 'Juliet chooses womanhood, and sexuality, and love and marriage, and therefore in the context of this play, she is forced to choose solitude and self-banishment' (p.207). She also contends that Romeo experiences significant self-growth in the play, but suggests 'when Romeo falls in love with Juliet, his language changes, and becomes sharply inventive, witty, and original' (p.192) – his evolution from stale clichés about Rosaline is a return to his authentic self, the kind of Romeo that Mercutio says he recognises. Garber contrasts this with the Friar and the Nurse as examples of 'dangerously static character[s]' (p.196), and believes this theme of old and staid versus new and revolutionary informs the end of the story. A trope of tragedy is that there should be change and development after the climactic event, but Garber considers the tragedy of Romeo and Juliet's ending to be that 'no one left alive onstage has understood the play' because as 'remnants of an older world of law' (p.212) they have failed to appreciate the necessity for new ways of thinking and behaving in a modern world.

Garber interprets the stagnation of old social orders and traditions as a key reason for the deaths in the play, and is of the view that both title characters undergo transformation as a result of their circumstances and choices.

Philosopher and literary scholar Paul A Kottman, however, 'contest[s] the notion that the "tragic" core of our modern subjectivity is rooted in a conflict between individual desires and the reigning demands of family, civic, and social norms shaping those desires' (Kottman 2012, p.5). He argues that modern audiences love the tragedy of this play because it shows a 'struggle for individual freedom and self-realization' (p.5) as the characters 'actively claim their separate individuality, their own freedom, in the only way they can – through each other' (p.6).

Kottman's reading identifies the play's ending as tragic but triumphant because the characters were not 'formed and thwarted' (p.38) by outside forces, but instead have attained personal freedom and self-actualisation from their determination to be together, even in death.

Two interpretations

Interpretation 1: *Romeo and Juliet* is a valuable and surprisingly modern take on romantic love.

Shakespeare's play *Romeo and Juliet* continues to be popular because it is one of the first 'modern' love stories. Juliet's father, Lord Capulet, insists his 'care hath been / To have her matched' (3.5.177–8) to Paris, but his sudden haste in arranging the marriage after Tybalt's death indicates this is more for his political and social advantage than for her benefit. Rather than follow traditional Elizabethan social expectations that daughters should obey their fathers, and that marriage is about allegiance rather than romance, the play values personal choice and a love match. Juliet should indeed be allowed to say 'I'll not wed, I cannot love; / I am too young, I pray you pardon me' (3.5.185–6).

This aligns with the modern view of equality between the sexes and marriage as an expression of love. When Romeo asks for consent to kiss Juliet's hand, then asserts, 'Thus from my lips, by thine, my sin is purged' (1.5.106), she responds archly, 'Then have my lips the sin that they have took' (1.5.107). Kisses are invited, exchanged and returned. This mutual respect is reflected in the couple's sonnet duets and the balance of listening and responding during their conversations. The Elizabethan world put men in a position of control in courtship, but today healthy romantic relationships are thought to be based on shared communication, respect and informed consent, as between Romeo and Juliet.

The play also champions romantic love above social and family duty. The Friar tells Romeo he hopes 'this alliance may so happy prove / To turn your households' rancour to pure love' (2.3.91–2). Many contemporary societies have come to value independence over family and social obligations, and Juliet's exhortation to Romeo, 'Deny thy father and refuse thy name' (2.2.34), for the sake of love, is in keeping with this.

Thus, for modern audiences, a key element of the play's tragedy is the fact these modern relationships could not be sustained in patriarchal

Elizabethan society. However, *Romeo and Juliet* remains beloved by contemporary audiences as it gives us hope that our world will continue evolving to allow everyone the freedom to choose love in whatever form it takes, and provide opportunities to build healthy relationships based on mutual respect, unfettered by family pressures or arbitrary social rules.

Interpretation 2: The depiction of romantic love in *Romeo and Juliet* is deeply problematic.

Despite its reputation as a beloved play about love, *Romeo and Juliet*'s depiction of 'true love' is fundamentally problematic for modern audiences. The relationship between the title characters is riven with inequality, impetuosity, undue influence and immaturity, and the tragic ending is ultimately a romanticisation of suicide.

A fundamental problem for contemporary audiences is Juliet's age – 'not fourteen' (1.3.15) – which in modern times is considered to be a child, and too young to be legally married in most countries. Indeed, pursuing her while almost an adult himself, the seventeen-year-old Romeo might now even be considered a sexual predator.

This imbalance of power is further exacerbated by their respective circumstances. With chasteness before marriage encouraged for young noblewomen, Juliet is inexperienced in social interactions with men and therefore highly vulnerable – it is likely she has never had a previous romantic encounter. Meanwhile, the audience first meets Romeo obsessing over Rosaline, and he later jokes lewdly with Mercutio about his 'pump [being] well flowered' (2.4.52). Even if Romeo is not sexually experienced, he has pursued love affairs and flirted with women, as evident in his suave greeting to Juliet: 'If I profane with my unworthiest hand / … / My lips … ready stand / To smooth … with a tender kiss' (1.5.92–5).

Social expectations of modern romantic relationships prioritise maturity, consistency and longevity, as per the Friar's advice to 'love moderately' as 'Too swift arrives as tardy as too slow' (2.6.14–15). However, these characters are indulging a teenage crush where they meet and kiss as strangers at a party. They are married (likely in order to have sex) within twenty-four hours. Their decisions are based on desire, and they make reckless choices about the lifelong contract of marriage. Moreover, when tragedy unfolds, they each blame the other: Romeo claims Juliet's 'beauty hath made [him] effeminate' (3.1.105), implying she bears some guilt for Mercutio's death, and Juliet calls him 'serpent heart, hid with a flow'ring face!' (3.2.73) to the Nurse upon learning that he has killed Tybalt.

However, there is an argument to be made for blaming the Friar for manipulating minors in his pastoral care. The Friar is eager that 'this alliance may so happy prove / To turn your households' rancour to pure love' (2.3.91–2) for personal, social and political reasons, and had he not agreed to officiate at their wedding, there might have been an opportunity for the couple to make less disastrous choices. As it is, the climax of the play is particularly unpalatable for modern audiences in suggesting the desirability of giving your life for love. The implication that it is better to sacrifice yourself for another than admit a relationship is untenable – and the implication that love can be made eternal through death – makes the tragic ending of *Romeo and Juliet* more distressing for its message than its events.

QUESTIONS & ANSWERS

This section focuses on your own analytical writing on the text, and gives you strategies for producing high-quality responses in your coursework and exam essays.

Essay writing – an overview

An essay on a literary work is a formal and serious piece of writing that presents your point of view on the text, usually in response to a given topic. Your 'point of view' in an essay is your interpretation of the meaning of the text's language, structure, characters, situations and events, supported by detailed analysis of textual evidence.

Analyse – don't summarise

In your essays it is important to avoid simply summarising what happens in a text.

- A **summary** is a description or paraphrase (retelling in different words) of the characters and events. For example: 'Macbeth has a horrifying vision of a dagger dripping with blood before he goes to murder King Duncan.'
- An **analysis** is an explanation of the real meaning or significance that lies 'beneath' the text's words (and images, for a film). For example: 'Macbeth's vision of a bloody dagger shows how deeply uneasy he is about the violent act he is contemplating, and conveys his sense that supernatural forces are impelling him to act.'

A limited amount of summary is sometimes necessary to let your reader know which part of the text you wish to discuss. However, always keep this to a minimum and follow it immediately with your analysis of what this part of the text is really telling us.

Plan your essay

Carefully plan your essay so that you have a clear idea of what you are going to say. The plan ensures that your ideas flow logically, that your argument remains consistent and that you stay on topic. An essay plan should be a list of **brief dot points** covering no more than half a page.

- Include your central argument or main contention – a concise statement of your overall response to the topic.
- Write three or four dot points for each paragraph, indicating the main idea and evidence/examples from the text. In your essay you will need to *expand* on these points and *analyse* the evidence.

Structure your essay

An essay is a complete, self-contained piece of writing. It has a clear beginning (the introduction), middle (several body paragraphs) and end (the last paragraph or conclusion). It must also have a central argument that runs throughout, linking each paragraph to form a coherent whole. See examples of introductions and conclusions in the 'Analysing a sample topic' and 'Sample answer' sections.

The introduction establishes your overall response to the topic. It includes your main contention and outlines the main evidence you will refer to in the course of the essay. Write your introduction *after* you have done a plan and *before* you write the rest of the essay.

The body paragraphs argue your case – they present evidence from the text and explain how this evidence supports your argument. Each body paragraph needs:

- a strong **topic sentence** (usually the first sentence) that states the main point being made in the paragraph
- **evidence** from the text, including some brief quotations
- **analysis** of the textual evidence, with **explanation** of its significance and how it supports your argument
- **links back to the topic** in one or more statements, usually towards the end of the paragraph.

Connect the body paragraphs so that your discussion flows smoothly. Use some linking words and phrases such as 'similarly' and 'on the other hand', though don't start every paragraph like this. Another strategy is to use a significant word from the last sentence of one paragraph in the first sentence of the next.

Use key terms from the topic – or synonyms for them – throughout, so the relevance of your discussion to the topic is always clear.

The conclusion ties everything together and finishes the essay. It includes strong statements that emphasise your central argument and provide a clear response to the topic.

Avoid simply restating the points made earlier in the essay – this will end on a very flat note and imply that you have run out of ideas and vocabulary. The conclusion should be a logical extension of what you have written, not just a repetition or summary of it. Writing an effective conclusion can be a challenge. Try using these tips:

- Start by linking back to the final sentence of the second-last paragraph, rather than leaping to your main contention straight away – this helps your writing to flow.
- Use synonyms and expressions with equivalent meanings to vary your vocabulary. This allows you to reinforce your line of argument without being repetitive.
- When planning your essay, think of one or two broad statements or observations about the text's wider meaning. These should be related to the topic and your overall argument. Keep them for the conclusion, since they will give you something 'new' to say but still follow logically from your discussion. The introduction will be focused on the topic, but the conclusion can present a wider view of the text.

Essay topics

1 How do the comic characters in *Romeo and Juliet* affect the tragic nature of the play?

2 To what extent does Romeo evolve over the course of the play?

3 How do modern ideas about love and romance influence our contemporary interpretations of the lovers' plight in *Romeo and Juliet*?

4 'A pair of star-crossed lovers take their life …'
Who or what is ultimately to blame for the deaths of Romeo and Juliet?

5 Mercutio, Paris, Friar Lawrence and the Prince are all connected to both families, and their different ways of dealing with the feud results in their own tragic outcomes.
Discuss.

6 How does the character of Juliet reflect the role of women in Elizabethan society?

7 If *Romeo and Juliet* has a moral, is it that we should follow the rules or rebel against them?

8 *Romeo and Juliet* suggests teenagers deserve more autonomy and choice within their families and society.
Discuss.

9 In the genre of tragedy, a central character is revealed to have a tragic flaw that brings about their downfall.
How does this idea apply to *Romeo and Juliet*?

10 Male aggression is the fundamental cause of the problems in Verona.
Discuss.

Vocabulary for writing on Romeo and Juliet

Allusion: an indirect reference to a myth, story or historical event outside the text. For example, 'Prince of Cats' (2.4.18) alludes to a medieval fable that has a feline character also called Tybalt.

Aside: a secret comment made by one character, only heard by the audience.

Dialogue: conversations between characters; spoken exchanges of ideas and opinions.

Epilogue: the concluding speech in a play.

Irony: a literary device in which there is a tension between what is said and what is meant, or between what is understood by a character and what is actually happening. For example, dramatic irony occurs when Romeo kills himself to join Juliet in death, but the audience knows that Juliet is still alive.

Metaphor: a description likening one thing to another without using comparative language, such as 'It is the east, and Juliet is the sun' (2.2.3).

Monologue: a significant speech by one character.

Motif: a recurring idea or image in a text, such as motifs of light and darkness.

Prologue: the opening speech in a play.

Simile: a description likening one thing to another using comparative language, such as 'The brightness of her cheek would shame those stars, / As daylight doth a lamp' (2.2.19–20).

Soliloquy: A monologue in which a character shares their thoughts and feelings with the audience.

Symbolism: an idea or an image that is loaded with specific meaning within a text. For example, the concept of 'poison' becomes a symbol in *Romeo and Juliet*, as an individual's actions, family pressure or societal expectations can be insidious and destructive.

Tragedy: a classic literary genre designed to evoke strong emotions, in which one or more characters experience terrible misfortune and exemplify human suffering.

Analysing a sample topic

Male aggression is the fundamental cause of the problems in Verona. Discuss.

This topic has three key components to evaluate:

- What **problems** are evident in this society?
- What examples of **male aggression** are portrayed?
- What is the **relationship** between these problems and these examples?

The topic assumes some understanding of gender roles and expectations in the world of the play, and is asking us to interpret the play through this lens.

The play presents multiple problems that we could consider in addressing this topic. These include:

- the historical **family feud** that continues to disrupt and threaten both the peace and people's lives in Verona
- Romeo and Juliet's **inability to love**, marry and continue to live in Verona without repercussions
- social expectations of **loyalty to family and friends** preventing characters from making their own choices or forcing them into unwanted situations, e.g. Mercutio fighting Tybalt, Juliet's parents demanding she wed Paris
- **gender expectations**, e.g. Juliet struggles for agency over her life; Romeo feels pressured into repressing his emotions and committing illegal acts.

Being able to demonstrate an understanding of the variety and extent of problems troubling this society will be important for this topic.

There are also numerous instances of male aggression in the play. These include:

- the opening street fight
- Tybalt's desire to attack Romeo at the party
- Tybalt officially challenging Romeo to a duel
- Tybalt attacking and killing Mercutio
- Romeo killing Tybalt
- Lord Capulet's threats of physical violence against Juliet
- Paris attacking Romeo, and Romeo killing Paris.

Being able to discuss the extent of aggression depicted in the play and how violent acts against others are presented as exclusive to men will be central in addressing this topic.

What, then, is the possible relationship between the violence male characters perpetrate and the inherent problems in this society? With topics such as this, it is always an option to argue against the proposition. However, examples and evidence collated for this particular topic offer more support for agreeing that male characters being aggressive does cause fundamental problems in the world of the play.

We could argue this by:

- analysing specific characters, or investigating how individual personalities and actions cause particular problems
- using key problems as a structure, or analysing which acts of aggression initiate or perpetuate them
- identifying possible causes for male aggression in this society, or correlating them with problems.

Our introduction will outline which approach we are taking to the topic, and present a contention that clearly answers the implied topic question: how and why is male aggression a fundamental cause of the problems in Verona?

Sample introduction

> In Shakespeare's *Romeo and Juliet*, Verona is depicted as a resolutely patriarchal society. Gender roles are strictly defined: women are expected to be passive and obedient, and men are pressured to be powerful and domineering. The aggression of male characters proves to be the fundamental cause of the problems in the play because the patriarchal need to maintain or acquire power, display strength or bravado in front of male peers or express emotion through rage or violence manifests in conflict and bloodshed. It is these actions that create and exacerbate the feud between the Capulets and the Montagues, prevent Romeo and Juliet from being together in life, and result in multiple deaths.

Body paragraph outline

Paragraph 1: Maintaining or acquiring power

- Patriarchs vying for power – most likely what sparks the feud. The feud causes civil unrest, resulting in the deaths of Tybalt, Mercutio and Paris, and is the reason Romeo and Juliet's relationship is fraught.
- Lord Capulet – threatening Juliet, and attempting to keep parental control and marry her off for his own gain, causes her to take desperate measures to avoid bigamy and eventually results in her death.

- Tybalt – looking to assert control over his enemies as the principal male heir of the Capulets causes the death of Mercutio, and his own death.

Paragraph 2: Displaying strength or bravado

- Tybalt – needing to prove himself to his uncle and enemies by inciting fights to show off physical skills and 'courage'. Arguably causes Romeo's exile by killing Mercutio and inciting revenge.
- Servants in opening street fight – more anxious to appear daring and aggressive than to actually cause violence, but their actions revive the feud into a 'new mutiny' (Prologue, line 3).
- Paris – foolish to provoke a fight with Romeo, but feels a need to prove himself. Causes Romeo to further despair, now twice a murderer, and to welcome death.

Paragraph 3: Expressing extreme emotion through rage or violence

- Paris – channels grief into violence because Veronese society does not facilitate men being emotional except through aggression.
- Lord Capulet – unable to deal with his anger and disappointment over Juliet's independence other than through verbal abuse.
- Romeo – provoked into fighting Tybalt by guilt over Mercutio's death, and fighting Paris when grieving for Juliet. Intensifies feud, prevents success of his marriage, and ultimately causes the death of his mother, his wife and himself.

Sample conclusion

The fundamental cause of the problems in Verona is shown convincingly to be the male aggression founded and fuelled by this patriarchal society. Even the most passive and peace-loving men, such as Benvolio and the Friar, are coerced into or succumb to street fights or violent words as a solution to the problems they face. Male characters in *Romeo and Juliet* feel compelled to pursue power and control, show off their masculine strength and physical skills, and convert 'feminine' emotions into aggression. The result is frequent acts of violence that disrupt the city, break the law, ruin relationships and lead to multiple tragic deaths.

SAMPLE ANSWER

How do the comic characters in *Romeo and Juliet* affect the tragic nature of the play?

Although the central plot of Shakespeare's *Romeo and Juliet* is focused on the lovers' tragic relationship, this is juxtaposed with scenes of witty banter, vulgar puns and high comedy. The comic characters of the Nurse, Mercutio, Peter and the Musicians serve not only to heighten the dramatic impact of the tragedy by providing a contrast, but also to explore other perspectives on the play's key themes of love and duty, and to represent the wider ramifications of Romeo and Juliet's fateful connection for Verona.

The Nurse often serves to disrupt or delay dramatic revelations with her chatter, for instance when the lovers' clandestine meeting is punctuated by her untimely interruptions, or when she makes excuses for taking her time to deliver news from Romeo: 'Do you not see that I am out of breath?' However, these interjections also offer insight into her character – as a hired companion, she is in a delicate position, poised between duty to her employers and love for Juliet. She conceivably realises more than she reveals about this fraught romantic encounter, and thus endeavours to obstruct the lovers' interactions at first. She does soon enough risk her career by facilitating the lovers' marriage to make her 'ladybird' happy, but she could still be having misgivings about betraying her superiors in her role as chaperone, which could explain her later prevarication.

The fact that the Nurse's own child, Susan, died in infancy explains why she is so sentimental about childhood memories. Her comic digressions take on pathos, and her loving devotion contrasts sharply with Juliet's relationship with her parents. Moreover, the Nurse's amusing but pragmatic views about sex and marriage offer a new perspective on both the play's central theme of love and the lovers' romantic decisions, for she jokes that getting married does not lessen women but makes them 'grow' larger, and suggests that bigamy is better than having 'no use of' an exiled husband. She intimates that love is not just ethereal, but about ongoing sexual needs, pregnancy and the future: a point of view the lovers have difficulty considering in their spontaneity and hasty passion.

Like the Nurse, Mercutio's comic dialogue creates both hilarity and anticipation in the play, as when his Queen Mab monologue becomes the turning point for Romeo and Juliet's fateful meeting. However, when making fun of his friend's sentimentality ('Romeo! humours! madman! passion! lover!') and insulting the Nurse ('A bawd, a bawd, a bawd! So ho!'), he also exemplifies gender issues in Verona that have affected the course of the couple's love. He considers Romeo mad for letting emotions rule him as a man, and disrespects the Nurse for seeking out a man she wants, which are also the attitudes of the two patriarchs in the play when evaluating the actions of their respective children. Part of the lovers' tragedy is that this world will not accept their non-conformity to the gender stereotypes Mercutio seems to perpetuate.

However, Mercutio also adds depth to the key themes of love and duty, not only in the sceptical, anti-romantic views he professes – 'If love be rough with you, be rough with love' – but also with his own unexpected representation of love and loyalty as a friend who is willing to self-sacrifice. His sexist words dismiss Romeo's pacifism as 'vile submission', but he acts to engage Tybalt's fury and save Romeo from fighting. Thus his death becomes a tragedy, where he identifies the underlying issue in Verona that infects and endangers all: 'A plague a'both houses!'

Finally, Peter and the Musicians' petty squabbles not only generate dramatic tension by comically delaying revelations of whether Juliet is actually dead and whether the Friar's plan will succeed, but also offer different social experiences of central events in the play. As other scenes with servants and working-class characters reveal, the plague of the family feud is affecting all layers of society. The class disparity, with the Musicians mostly concerned about whether they can 'stay [for] dinner', exposes the unconscious entitlement of these 'noble' characters damaging Verona by indulging their own selfish wants and needs.

The genre of tragedy traditionally provides catharsis for an audience – a safe and healthy way to experience and process extreme emotions. Shakespeare understood the need to balance anger, anxiety and grief with the life-affirming emotions of joy, amusement and ridicule. His comic characters in *Romeo and Juliet* serve to heighten the impact of the tragedy by creating anticipation and contrast, but also represent the wider impact of the issues affecting Verona and offer new understandings of significant themes, while demonstrating their own complex personalities and motivations.

REFERENCES & READING

Text

Smith, R (ed.) 2014, *Romeo and Juliet*, 4th edn, Cambridge School Shakespeare series, Cambridge University Press, Cambridge.

References and reading

Aristotle 1996 (composed c.330 BCE), *Poetics*, Penguin Books, London.

Bloom, H 1999, *Shakespeare: The Invention of the Human*, Fourth Estate, London.

Bloom, H (ed.) 2010, 'Introduction', *Bloom's Guides: William Shakespeare's Romeo and Juliet*, Infobase Publishing, New York.

Garber, M 2004, *Shakespeare After All*, Anchor Books, New York.

Halio, JL (ed.) 1996, *Shakespeare's Romeo and Juliet: Texts, Contexts, and Interpretations*, University of Delaware Press, New York.

Kottman, PA 2012, 'Defying the stars: tragic love as the struggle for freedom in *Romeo and Juliet*', *Shakespeare Quarterly*, vol. 63, no. 1, Spring, pp.1–38.

Ridgway, C 2024, 'The Tilbury Speech', *The Elizabeth Files*, https://www.elizabethfiles.com/resources

Smith, RM 1948, 'Three interpretations of *Romeo and Juliet*', *The Shakespeare Association Bulletin*, vol. 23, no. 2, pp.59–77.

Film and video

Shakespeare in Love 1998, dir. John Madden, Universal Pictures. Starring Gwyneth Paltrow, Joseph Fiennes and Geoffrey Rush.

Upstart Crow 2016–17, dir. Matt Lipsey / Richard Boden, BBC. Starring David Mitchell, Gemma Whelan, Rob Rouse and Liza Tarbuck. See season 1, episode 1, 'Star Crossed Lovers', and season 2, episode 6, 'Sweet Sorrow'.

William Shakespeare's Romeo + Juliet 1996, dir. Baz Luhrmann, 20th Century Fox. Starring Leonardo DiCaprio, Claire Danes, John Leguizamo and Harold Perrineau.

Websites

Romeo and Juliet 2024, Royal Shakespeare Company, https://www.rsc.org.uk/romeo-and-juliet/

Romeo and Juliet 2024, Shakespeare's Globe, https://2019.playingshakespeare.org/

Romeo and Juliet 2024, The Folger Shakespeare Library, https://www.folger.edu/explore/shakespeares-works/romeo-and-juliet/

Shakespedia 2024, Shakespeare Birthplace Trust, https://www.shakespeare.org.uk/explore-shakespeare/shakespedia/